PARENTING SCHOOL-AGE TWiNS AND MULTiPLES

PARENTING SCHOOL-AGE TWiNS AND MULTiPLES

CHRISTINA BAGLIVI TINGLOF

New York   Chicago   San Francisco   Lisbon   London   Madrid   Mexico City
Milan   New Delhi   San Juan   Seoul   Singapore   Sydney   Toronto

The *McGraw-Hill* Companies

Library of Congress Cataloging-in-Publication Data

Tinglof, Christina Baglivi .
    Parenting school-age twins and multiples / Christina Baglivi Tinglof.
        p.   cm.
    Includes bibliographical references and index.
    ISBN 0-07-146902-8 (alk. paper)
      1. Parenting.   2. Twins—Psychology.   3. Only child—Psychology.
    4. Parenting.   I. Title.

    HQ755.8.T55   2007
    649'.144—dc22   2006027151

1 2 3 4 5 6 7 8 9 10 11 12 13 14 15 16 17 18 19   FGR/FGR   0 9 8 7 6

ISBN-13: 978-0-07-146902-9
ISBN-10:   0-07-146902-8

McGraw-Hill books are available at special quantity discounts to use as premiums and sales promotions, or for use in corporate training programs. For more information, please write to the Director of Special Sales, Professional Publishing, McGraw-Hill, Two Penn Plaza, New York, NY 10121-2298. Or contact your local bookstore.

This book is printed on acid-free paper.

To my family. What a great ride.

Contents

Foreword

In my thirty years of research with multiple-birth families, I have been fortunate to be involved in two longitudinal studies of the development of twins throughout childhood. These have convinced me of the power of early events that may shape the life course of twin pairs and the relationship of the young people to each other as they move into adulthood. Explaining such events is one particular strength of this book as it traces twins and higher multiples through preschool, elementary school, and high school into college and adulthood. And this is not just a book for parents. It is equally relevant for other relatives such as grandparents and also for teachers, so that they can appreciate their role in how the children finally emerge into adulthood.

WHERE HAS THE INFORMATION COME FROM?

One achievement of this book comes from the ability of the author to interweave two sources of information: interviews with more than forty families and the scientific literature. She overlays this with her experiences as a mother of twins plus a mother of the often overlooked sibling of twins. Academic researchers often fail to recognize the wealth of information that can come from parents. This is especially so in the case of multiple-birth families, where so much of the data gathered has been highly quantitative and based on genetic research and has not ventured into what life is like for the multiples and their parents, siblings, and teachers. This has been brought home to me clearly in a study we have been doing recently of families where one twin has ADHD and the other does not. None of our formal psychological measurements really got at what life was like for the non-ADHD twin. That came out in their dialogue when they spoke of their embarrassment at some of the behaviors of their cotwin at school but also the bond between them despite these hassles.

The text uses powerful verbal images to capture some of the things unique to the multiple-birth family. I can think of no better illustration of the competition between twins than the example of the boy who screamed out, "I've won, I've won" at the end of a footrace when in fact he had not won but had come in second to last. It was his twin who was last. Examples such as this provide great insight into what is in the mind of a twin.

Along with this comes very insightful and thorough explanation of the twin research literature, aided by the author's skills as a journalist to translate the often dry prose of the academic. My own group's work has been used quite extensively, and I have to admit there were times when I read a section and wondered, "Did we really find that?" Yes we had, but we had not expressed it so clearly. I particularly appreciate the recognition of the work of Helen Koch in Chicago and Rene Zazzo in France, two people whose contributions to understanding the world of twins have not received the audience they deserve.

Rene Zazzo's idea of the "couple effect" was very insightful but long overlooked because so little of his work was available in English. Helen Koch's "prima donna" effect is hugely important also but has been neglected in recent years. Though their work only features in this book in the discussion of adolescence, I recommend every reader reflect on how it fits with so many multiples from preschool onward as they work together to get attention ("prima donnas") or seek to distance themselves and exaggerate what differences may lie between themselves ("the couple effect").

In identifying that life was different for twins if they were identical or nonidentical, female or male, the same or opposite sex, Helen Koch made a major contribution that is too often missed by families who seek guidance from other books on multiples—namely, she documented that not all kids and families are the same. Constantly throughout this book we are reminded that not all multiple-birth families are the same and that what works for one family may not work for the next. So while this book may not give you the precise recipe to sort out your own family, it does give you the ingredients that may be combined in the most appropriate way to give you greater understanding of your own family's dynamics.

INDIVIDUALITY AND COMPETITION

One point I had overlooked in Mary Rosambeau's *How Twins Grow Up* but that took my breath away when cited here was that on average twins in the United Kingdom first spent two or more nights apart at the age of fourteen, compared with age nine for nontwin siblings. (Here the United States may be different. The idea of children going away from home for a significant part of the summer, far less going without their twin, is unusual outside the United States.) This is a real challenge to the argument that twins experience the same range of environments as pairs of single-born siblings.

What I really liked about the book was the way the challenge between individuality and the power of being multiples was woven through the text. As the author points out, comparisons between multiples begin at birth (if not before, given some of the recent Italian ultrasound work) and can shape attitudes toward the individual twins and the relationship between them throughout their lives. I endorse the firm approach taken with relatives who may want to compare the children. It certainly may ruffle the feathers of a grandparent or other relative to be told to stop doing so, but it is the long-term interest of the multiples that matters, not the short-term emotions of the adults concerned.

But firm talk is not just for relatives. The message comes through clearly that life is not fair. Twins and higher multiples cannot be isolated from differences between them, for example when one but not the other(s) gets a scholarship or some other recognition. The book makes it clear that parents cannot and should not feel guilty about this. Indeed, if anything the opposite is the case, and parents should feel guilty if they try to protect their children by refusing to acknowledge real differences between them.

IS THIS BOOK RELEVANT
OUTSIDE NORTH AMERICA?

Every author (and even more so every publisher) wants the biggest market for a new book. So does this book translate outside North America? Beyond such obvious issues as the perennial inability of Americans to spell *Mum*, I think every family will find examples to relate to, irrespective of where the family lives. That is due in no small part to the author's efforts to use international work, such as that of Mary Rosambeau in the United Kingdom and Rene Zazzo in France, the many twin research groups in Scandinavia, and our own efforts in Australia.

This does not mean differences between countries are absent. This is particularly the case in the vexed area of whether or not to separate multiples in school. Our own work in Australia on this topic began almost twenty years ago, with the United Kingdom initiatives by my colleague Pat Preedy starting a few years later. In 1990, the education department of one Australian state, Queensland, issued a directive to all schools that there must be no rigid policy on the separation of multiples and that parents should be consulted. Our website Twins and Multiples (twinsandmultiples.org), launched in 2001, included a draft policy for schools to consider in the placement of multiples. So it is sad that in 2005, Minnesota found it necessary to pass a bill giving parents a voice in the school placement of their children, an initiative that other U.S. states are now adopting.

The author has done an excellent job of summarizing the issues around whether or not twins should be separated, including the two recent studies from the United Kingdom and the Netherlands that use longitudinal data to show there are no disadvantages in keeping twins together in elementary school and possibly some advantages. This brings me to my final point: How can the messages of this book reach those who need to know?

THE CHALLENGE: HOW TO GET THE MESSAGE OUT

All the way through this book at the back of my mind was the question of whether the "right" people will read it. Of course parents will, but what about other relatives? Will the grandparent who has a "favorite" twin recognize his or her own situation and change his or her ways? Will the school administrator appreciate the reasoned section on schooling and recognize that no rigid policy will fit all sets of multiples? There is a great deal of wisdom from families and from researchers packed in here. All of us who work with or care for multiples need to do what we can to get the message out to improve the lives of those multiples being born and reared in the twenty-first century. And this book encapsulates the most recent thinking for these children and their families.

The message that needs to get out is more than simply how to cope with the extra challenges of raising multiples. It can be hard work, and there are dilemmas and decisions that families with single-born children never have to make. This book helps you make more informed decisions when such situations arise. But the book is positive and one also gets a good sense of the plusses about being a twin or higher multiple. Families with newborn multiples or even those still expecting their multiples will benefit from reading this book and appreciating the joy of multiples that can be theirs forever.

> **—David A. Hay,** Professor of Psychology,
> Curtin University, Western Australia;
> National Patron, Australian Multiple Birth
> Association; Associate Editor (Child Development), *Twin Research and Human Genetics*

Acknowledgments

I'd like to extend my sincerest gratitude to all those who helped make this book a wonderful reality. Many thanks to Dr. David A. Hay for penning the book's foreword and offering valuable feedback. Thanks to my editors, past and present, Michele Matrisciani and Deborah Brody. To my agent, Betsy Amster, I couldn't have done it without you. A special nod to my husband, Kevin, for taking on extra family responsibilities during the length of this project. And thanks to all those parents who so graciously gave their time to fill out questionnaires or spoke with me directly including Cheryl Feldman, Jan Meyers, Chris, Sandy Davis, Adrianne Austin, Mary E., Gretchen S. Pretty, Pam Heestand, Alicia Gutierrez, Julie Dupré Gilman, Susan and John Leahy, Renee Hald, Oma Jane Woods, Steve and Betty Bullington, Amy Mahaffey, Jeannette, Jim, Rick, Nancy Johnson and family, Mary W. Pasciuto, Jennifer Reed, Lucia Shugart, Linda M. Yaffee, Donna May Lyons, the Boretz family, Sue Bernier, Martha Slater, Ann Owens, Julie Seely, Kimberley Farrar, Laurie Moore, Christine Kumler, Donna Fredericks, Linda Gliner, MyrtleBeth, Julie McCarron, Amber Radunz, Heidi Snyder, Juliann Lipski, Christy Helvajian, Sheila Kroll, Sabrina Sanchez, Robin Bortoli, the Hicks family of Prattsville, and to those who wished to remain anonymous.

Introduction

You finally retired that double stroller (or maybe you're making room in the attic to stow your trio of high chairs), and double-duty diaper changes are a thing of the past. Congratulations. You did it! You survived the first few years of multiple madness where a good night's sleep seemed nearly impossible and when one twin started to run one way, his cotwin inevitably ran in the opposite direction. While I'm sure you're relieved on some level that those hectic days are a thing of the past, you're a bit sad, too. After all, they were darn cute, weren't they? Two times the love and two times the charm. Remember all the enthusiastic comments you'd get from people passing by as you strolled through the neighborhood with your two cherubs beaming from the comfort of their tandem stroller? You felt proud if just a bit sick of hearing the same old remarks like, "Are they twins?"

But now your multiples are growing up, and fast! Things are changing rapidly, too, for both you and your twins. You're no longer frantically asking, "How do I nurse them both at the same time?" or "What do I do when they both cry at once?" Now you want to know if it's a good idea to separate your multiples into different classrooms once they hit kindergarten, how you can encourage each child to grow into a unique individual while maintaining a strong intratwin bond, or even if they should share the same bedroom. Plus, your twins themselves are coming to you with questions that parents of singletons rarely deal with, such as, "Why can't I go with him to Billy's house? He's my friend, too" or "It's not fair that he got the science award and I didn't." You desperately want to say the right thing to the twin who feels disappointment but at the same time not diminish the happiness or accomplishments of the other. Yet how can you do both simultaneously?

In recent years, as twinning and multiple births continue to rise, more and more books on the care and rearing of young multiples are hitting store shelves, but that's old news to you. You've been there and done that. There's also plenty of parenting wisdom available on raising singleton children, but that doesn't quite fit your family's profile either. Other parents may try to tell you that their close-in-age children are just like having multiples. (Haven't we all heard that comment at least once?) You just smile, knowing full well it's anything but, especially when your multiples were very young and their needs were not only constant but also in unison.

Raising multiples is indeed very different than raising non-twin siblings no matter how close in age they are. Unlike single-born children, multiples are conceived and come into this world as a pair or a group, leading many to speculate that a strong bond blossoms in utero. During the first few years of life, multiples demand more attention from their parents than a single-born child, and yet at the same time, they must learn to accept their parents' divided attention. They also grow up and develop in the presence of a same-age sibling, reaching many developmental milestones simultaneously. This "couple effect" can have great implications on their relationship as they mature. Although many multiples enjoy their connection and friendship and take pride in their similar appearance, hobbies, or interests, others do not and instead take on specific opposite characteristics just to distinguish themselves from the other. Just as you knew that caring for infant and toddler twins would be different than nurturing a singleton, raising school-age multiples has its own set of unique challenges as well as rewards.

There are some well-documented differences between singletons and twins. For instance, did you know that multiples are more likely than single-born children to experience language problems or delayed speech, often resulting in reading difficulties once they hit school, which in turn may contribute to an increase in attention-deficit/hyperactivity disorder (ADHD)? Because of their close interaction with each other, they may experience social situations differently than single-born children too, such as being compared to each other more frequently or viewed and sometimes treated as a single entity. Yet through it all, it's the twin or multiple bond that keeps multiples strong in good times as well as bad and the rest of us marveling at their union, how they take genuine pleasure being in the company of each other.

So where can you go to get the answers to all these pressing new concerns? Now parents with older twins and higher-order multiples are getting their due. This book was written exclusively for parents like you who are passing on all that double equipment—the two cribs, the double high chairs, both trikes—and moving on. In this book, you won't see a discussion on putting young multiples on a schedule (these days, your busy kids probably have you on one) or tips on potty training two or more reluctant toddlers at once. Nope. Instead *Parenting School-Age Twins and Multiples* delves into new territory—life with multiples between the ages of five and eighteen—with a whole host of new tips and solutions to all your puzzling parenting questions. For instance, if your multiples are constant rivals, how can you help them to live harmoniously with each other? If your twins are very close, will that affect their individuality, or will it actually help them to become more sociable? What do you do if one twin is ready for kindergarten and the other isn't—should you wait another year so they can attend together? And what about the number one question every parent with multiples ultimately asks: should you separate them into different classrooms? It's such an emotionally charged topic that nearly everyone from the school principal to your next-door neighbor has an opinion. What about adolescence: Is it really different for multiples than singletons? What happens to opposite-sex multiples, boy-girl twins, for instance, when she hits puberty well before her brother? And how does having a nontwin sibling either younger or older than your multiples affect the family dynamics? All of these important questions are thoroughly examined and answered, offering parents of older twins reassurance, advice, and ideas for better living.

Thanks to hundreds of large, in-depth published studies as well as the clinical work of psychologists, educators, and scientists who specialize in the field of twin research, we're learning more and more about the experiences of being a multiple. But getting the answers to parents' questions took a bit of detective work. I scrutinized volumes of these analytical texts, books on multiples, and published research studies and boiled down the statistical and technical information into a language that we can all understand. (Although I only highlighted the results, you can read these published studies in their entirety yourself. All the books, periodicals, and research papers I consulted are noted in the Bibliography section in the back of the book for your reference.)

In addition to the scientific research, *Parenting School-Age Twins and Multiples* offers the insight of dozens of parents with older twins and triplets who have seen it all, the good and the not-so-good. I sent out more than one hundred detailed surveys to parents asking them about their experiences in parenting multiples. Forty-four surveys came back—the parents of a total of ninety-five multiples participated in all (several families had more than one set of twins). The zygosity (genetic relationship between twins and triplets) of this large sampling of multiples is as follows: sixteen identical males, twelve identical females, ten nonidentical males, eighteen nonidentical females, twenty-six opposite-sex twins, two pairs of twins whose zygosity is unknown (one pair of same-sex females and one pair of same-sex males), and three sets of triplets. The sampling ranged in age from six years old to thirty-three, with a mean age of thirteen. The parents' responses to my questions were very candid, and the ones included in this book will speak directly to you and address many of your current concerns.

Most surveys were so interesting that it was difficult to choose which quotes to include in the book. Two of the more intriguing ones came from parents who didn't know the zygosity of their twins. "We didn't have the test done to determine zygosity, but my doctor said he was 85 percent sure they were not identical," one mom said. "They looked exactly the same to me as newborns but began to show differences as they got older." Even now at age thirteen, her boys still have the same hair texture and color and the same eye color. They've always been within a pound of each other in weight and within an inch of each other in height.

"I'm curious to know but I don't want to fork over the money for the test!" joked the second mom, whose teenage daughters also look very much alike. "I did examine the placenta when they were born, and the nurse said that even though it looked like only one, they could have fused together." (It's important to note, however, that looks can be deceiving, as 25 to 30 percent of twins with separate placentas can be identical and 20 percent of twins with only one placenta can be fraternal. Furthermore, although the only true way to determine zygosity is through diagnostic testing, study after study concludes that a parent's "best guess" of zygosity is a whopping 95 percent accurate. Maybe mother does know best!)

And why is knowing your twins' zygosity important? Aside from medical considerations (in the unlikely event that if an organ or tissue transplant is needed for one, an identical sibling would be a perfect match), there are many characteristics that are intrinsic to twin type, and knowing the true zygosity can help explain your twins' relationship more fully. For instance, if your twins seem very close, sharing nearly all of their friends even through their middle school years, and find it difficult to be apart from one another, you can rest assured that this is perfectly normal behavior for identical twins, whose shared DNA accounts for their tight bond. And armed with the information put forth in this book about the nature of identical multiples, you can gently guide them on their journey toward individuality.

Although these surveys are far from the controlled studies of twins that I reference in the book, they did offer wonderful insight into the life of an older multiple. Choosing an interesting cross section of multiples—from twins who were just starting out in school, to those in high school, the college years, and even young adulthood—provided an understanding of the unique experiences of parenting multiples at various ages and developmental stages. The parents with young children, for instance, were in the thick of classroom separation issues, the lone birthday party invitation, and so on. On the other hand, while the moms and dads of high school and college-age twins had distant recollections of those early years, they were aptly able to illuminate the challenges of the teen years such as lack of privacy, the onset of puberty, and the struggle for individuality and resulting competitiveness. Having a wide span of ages, therefore, gave the overall responses and subsequent counsel more profoundness.

At this time, few published studies exist on the cognitive and social development of higher-order multiples (although I'm sure that with the continued rise in triplets and quads more will follow in the coming years). I have, however, highlighted specific information that I did find pertaining to parenting higher-order multiples. In addition, a reader with triplets or quads can easily extrapolate a wide range of help from the text, even when it's not higher-order multiple specific.

I hope you'll use this book as a guide to better understanding the life of being a twin, triplet, or quad. Yet I'd like to stress that although the text discusses many challenges that are unique to school-age multiples such as having a higher incidence of reading problems or grappling in unique ways to develop individual identity, and may make some readers uncomfortable with worry, not all multiples will struggle. In fact, most, even with these hardships, will do just fine in the end. The information offered here is meant to enlighten you. Knowledge is empowering. In addition, as you read through the chapters, you'll find a variety of solutions, some of which may speak directly to your family situation, some of which may not fit your parenting style at all. Parenting is never a one-size-fits-all scenario. What's the norm for one family may be unheard-of in another. Above all, take your cues from your children themselves. They'll let you know if there's a problem—you just need to pay attention, look for the signs, and step in accordingly.

Whether you're a parent of toddler twins curious to learn about what you can do now to help your multiples get the best possible foot up or you're a seasoned parent who's just in need of some reassurance that all is well with your teenagers despite their raging hormones, *Parenting School-Age Twins and Multiples* has what you need. I hope you'll refer to this book often to assist you in building healthy multiple relationships and inspire you to be the best parent you can be.

1

Understanding the Intratwin Relationship

This year, as I watch my nonidentical twin sons pass their tenth year together as a team, I continue to marvel at their relationship with a bit of awe and yes, even a bit of envy. I wonder what it must be like to have a best friend who's also your sibling, and a twin sibling at that. Being a twin, triplet, or quadruplet is different than being singleton siblings, even if the siblings are close in age. Not only do multiples grow and develop side-by-side sharing many common interests, but comparisons made between them are more obvious (and often more destructive) than they are with different-age siblings. Most likely none of us shared the womb with our best friend either, nor did we grow up in the same home sharing a birthday! Yet these and many more components make up the differences among a close friendship, siblingship, and a twinship.

When people ask me to describe my sons' bond, I answer that they're the best of friends and the worst of enemies— they're two sides of the same coin. For instance, nothing warms me as much as watching them leave the school yard together at the end of the day. I'm still amazed that they walk side by side whispering to each other about the day's events. Yet it's not more than ten minutes after they enter our front door that they are physically and verbally sparring with each other over who gets to play PlayStation first or who gets to eat the last chocolate chip cookie.

As parents of multiples, you've witnessed firsthand that the relationship between multiples is unique and often very special indeed. In this first chapter, we'll examine the twin or multiple bond—where and when it begins, how it differs for each subgroup of multiples, how it evolves throughout their lives, as well as the facts and the fiction that surround it.

THE SIX SUBGROUPS OF TWINNING

How many times has a stranger who's spied your double stroller stopped you in a shopping mall? After the requisite "Are they twins?" inevitably these well-meaning busybodies get to the ultimate question: "Are they identical or fraternal?" We've all been taught to refer to twins as either of these two names. Yet did you know that's only part of the story? Within these two categories there are six subcategories. First, a quick refresher course in the biology of twinning: When a single sperm fertilizes one egg and it splits into two separate zygotes, we say that the twins are identical, or to be more scientific, monozygotic (or MZ for short). These twins share the exact same genetic makeup (DNA) and often many physical, psychological, and behavior traits. If, on the other hand, two different sperm fertilize two different eggs simultaneously (or pretty darn close to it), we say they're nonidentical twins, dizygotic (DZ), more commonly known as fraternal twins. They share approximately 50 percent of their DNA—the same as any nontwin siblings—and often look and act nothing alike.

It's also been theorized that an additional twin type exists that is identical in maternal genes (the egg splits before fertilization) but different in paternal genes (the separated eggs are fertilized by two different sperm). This unofficial twin type is called polar-body twins, or half-identical twins because each twin has 50 percent matching genes from the mother and about 25 percent matching genes from the two different sperm. In the end, these children share approximately 75 percent of their DNA—about 25 percent more than fraternal twins, accounting for why polar-body twins often look so much alike.

One mom told me she's convinced her daughters fall within this hypothetical twin category. "We tested Sam and Alex when they were two and a half because the doctors at birth thought they were fraternal but they looked and acted identical. The tests came back fraternal—two of thirteen markers were different," she said. "I knew there was no way that they could be totally fraternal because there were too many similarities between them." For instance, both were born with the same physical problems. They learned to walk on the same day and both have a webbed toe on their left foot and the same color eyes. They both started wearing glasses when they were two years old. Today, at age fifteen, the girls still react to most situations exactly the same, having identical likes and dislikes both in their hobbies and in their choice of high school boys! And finally, they reached puberty almost simultaneously, starting their periods one week apart.

So how many of these mysterious polar-body twins roam the world? It's nearly impossible to determine because currently there's no DNA test to validate this intriguing theory. At this time, polar-body or half-identical is not considered a true twin type.

In addition to the identical and nonidentical classifications, researchers have divided twins into six subgroups: identical

From One Parent to Another

"Because Matthew, Claire, and Gregory (trizygotic) are triplets, the dynamics of 'ally versus enemy' changes on a daily basis. One day the boys are best friends with my daughter 'odd man out.' Then the next day, one son and my daughter could be playing a game together while the other boy is off on his own reading a book. Their fights are tremendous, but they are a united force to be reckoned with if an outsider crosses any one of them!"

females (MZf), identical males (MZm), nonidentical same-sex females (DZSSf), nonidentical same-sex males (DZSSm), and opposite-sex pairs (DZOSm and DZOSf, male and female respectively). And why is this important, you ask? Not only is it more accurate (after all, the word *identical* indicates that the pair is interchangeable rather than the two separate individuals that they are) but it also helps us analyze each subgroup's unique set of characteristics. (Besides, it's a lot quicker to type or write DZOSf than opposite-sex female!) Throughout this book, you'll see these terms and symbols used jointly along with the more common "identical" and "nonidentical" and fraternal classifications.

Triplets, on the other hand, fall into three categories: all identical (monozygotic), where one egg is fertilized by one sperm and then splits into two separate zygotes and then one splits yet again; two identical and one fraternal (dizygotic), where two ovum are fertilized by two separate sperm and then only one splits yet again into two different zygotes; and finally, all fraternal (or trizygotic), where three eggs are fertilized by three different sperm.

Yet do all these subgroups really differ from each other? In the end, kids are kids, and multiples are no different—they fight and love, compete, and cooperate just like every other child on the block. Although it's never a good idea to pigeonhole any child into a role—especially multiples—there are some subtle differences among the six twin and three triplet subgroups worth exploring. You may already have witnessed many of these idiosyncrasies in your own children. Furthermore, it is a different experience being a twin or triplet in an identical set where someone else looks and often acts exactly like you, a nonidentical set where the need to be seen as an individual can be strong and lead to rivalry, especially once you hit puberty, and in an opposite-sex pair where birth order means little and whether you're a boy or girl means everything.

Twin Subgroups: How Different Are They?

Differences among the six subgroups can be hard to quantify, but studies have been done throughout the years. Psychologist Helen Koch from the University of Chicago, for example, studied ninety pairs of twins (all with similar backgrounds) equally divided by subgroup, as well as a singleton control group. Always fascinated by twins, Koch wanted to try to classify variations in zygosity as well as differences between twins and singletons. In other words, she wanted to know if there were marked contrasts between MZ and DZ twins, what psychological and social effects twins have on each other, and if growing up as a single child is any different than growing up as a twin. Although she conducted her research back in the mid-1960s, she's still considered the leading pioneer in twin research. Her studies have never been repeated to such an extent, and most of the results are still valid today. Most important, though, her work offers us an appreciation for the "twin situation," those interesting dilemmas—the quest for individual identity, twin competition and cooperation—that multiples experience not by any other fault than being born with a same-age partner.

It should come as no surprise, for instance, that her research found that twins in general are closer to each other than singletons of the same age—they play together more often, share toys, clothes, and friends more easily than single-born children in the same family. Identical twins (MZ), on the whole, are a closer, more tightly knit subgroup than same-sex fraternal twins (DZSS), and they in turn are closer than opposite-sex twins (DZOS).

In her research, for instance, Koch compared identical girls (MZf) with same-sex fraternal girls (DZSSf) and found that the former group shared possessions more freely with each other and made less of a fuss when an item was borrowed without permission, shared more of each other's friends, and preferred to play with their cotwins rather than play alone. Could this closeness be explained by their shared gene pool? Or could it be that parents expect MZ twins to be closer than same-sex fraternal twins and therefore treat identical twins more uniformly? It's impossible to tell.

MZf (identical females) and DZSSf (fraternal females) seem to gravitate toward the attention that their twinship gives them, often using it to their social advantage. Adolescent MZf can be especially guilty of this characteristic at times, often highlighting their similarities in the hopes of retaining friends and their popularity. (This is called the prima donna effect and will be discussed at length in Chapter 7, "When They

Reach Puberty.") DZSSf (fraternal females) often develop a deep friendship but can become friendly rivals as they approach high school when issues of independence surface and outside friendships can compromise the union. Yet these girls still feel let down when their cotwins don't offer the companionship and encouragement that they feel the relationship requires. This is different from MZf, who often offer support naturally without any urging from parents.

Another interesting distinction between the subgroups lies within identical males (MZm) and same-sex fraternal males

> ### From One Parent to Another
>
> "Victoria and Kate (MZf) are truly the best of friends and worst of enemies—often simultaneously. They are together, mainly by choice, every waking moment of their day. They have separate bedrooms and sleep apart, which accounts for the longest separation they ever have. While watching TV, always in the same room, they will sit on the same sofa with their limbs intertwined and think nothing of it. Then, if they begin to fight and I ask them to separate, they think I'm the one who's crazy."

(DZSSm). Koch found that the former group was less competitive than the latter group since identical twins usually act as a united front rather than put stress on the relationship by disagreeing. (Koch found very little difference in female twins' competitiveness between MZf and DZSSf, however.) She also found that MZm were more shy and socially hesitant and less talkative than both DZSSm and same-sex singletons. But how much of that, she asked, was due to the intricate workings of their intratwin relationship? Their ability to instinctively know the inner qualities of their cotwin? Identical boys seem, too, to have the strongest relationship with their fathers since there is often a lack of competition for attention between identical males.

Other research has found that nonidentical same-sex boys are more mischievous both at school and at home, perhaps

---

From One Parent to Another

"Evan and Hope (DZOS) have a close bond, although this does not always manifest itself positively—one moment they're bosom pals and the next sworn enemies. Evan is the physically stronger of the two, and this has long been a source of contention to his sister, leading her, in my view, to hone some pretty admirable verbal skills and manipulative abilities from an early age. As a result, she is probably now 'the boss' of the two most of the time. Evan is often happy to go along with what she wants to do (the bosom pal moments), although he does occasionally rebel (the sworn enemy moments). This has us concerned that he's a little overdependent on his sister and has shaped our approach to both their schooling and their extracurricular activities, particularly in the last year or so. Hope is gradually becoming more attuned to her brother's need to shine and does now often notice what he does well and comments on it."

---

explaining why twin boys experience more attention-deficit problems than any other twin subgroup as well as singletons. Parents, too, find twin boys to be more trying than any other subgroup, but that shouldn't come as a surprise to anyone who has raised a house full of males! Koch found these boys to be more aggressive yet higher in leadership skills—they were more assertive of their rights than MZm twins.

Koch found opposite-sex pairs to have the most interesting characteristics, namely, that by the time they reach the school years, the females were viewed as more socially dominant than their brothers (more on how their twinship can affect the school years in Chapter 4, "Multiples and Education"). Many of the boys in this subgroup seemed aware of this assertive role that their sisters played, and although they liked being catered to, most also reported that they did not enjoy being in a subordinate position once they reached the school years. As a result, it sometimes caused stress in their union.

Although these idiosyncrasies have been documented in many respected research studies, the results may not match your family situation. Not all opposite-sex preschool twins will have a dominant female and a submissive male, for instance. Not all identical twins will cooperate fully with each other, and not every nonidentical male set will experience attention problems or act out in school. Every family, and every multiple, is different. Yet in the forty-four surveys I collected, compiling

Mirror Image Twins

Mirror image twins—multiples who have many inherited and physical traits on opposite sides of each other—were used to help establish twin type because it was thought that only mirror image twins were identical. Today there are more accurate tests to determine twins' zygosity, plus there's a small amount of speculation that nonidentical twins can be mirror images as well. Researchers believe mirror imaging happens in approximately one-quarter of MZ twins when the ovum splits later in the embryonic stage, after the right and left sides of what would have been a single person have been established. Some scientists have even considered that left-handed singletons are the survivors of a "vanishing twin" pair.

Are your twins mirror images of each other? Currently, there's no test to prove this interesting twist of nature; confirmation is based solely on observation. So what are some of the reversed patterns indicating mirror image twins?

- Opposite handedness (one child is right-handed, the other left).
- Opposite hair whorls (look at the crown of the head to see if the hair follicles grow clockwise or counterclockwise).
- In very rare cases, organs located on the opposite side of the body!

more than ninety-five multiples in all, the majority fall within these twin parameters. Most parents of boy-girl sets, for instance, spoke of their daughters acting as spokesperson for the pair during the early childhood years; middle and high school, same-sex fraternal twins exhibited more of a need to be seen as different from each other (which at times manifested itself through rivalry) than identical twins; and finally, all parents of identical twins described their multiples as having a tight union, even those MZ multiples who are now adults.

THE TWIN BOND

By nature of their twinship, multiples are "high-access" siblings. That is, they spend a lot of time together during the early formative years, often encouraged by their parents. As a result of an early, prolonged exposure to each other, and often without much input of other single-born siblings, twins and higher-order multiples develop an influential and intense sibling alliance. They have great impact and power on each other's personality and feelings. Although this relationship is most influential during childhood and adolescence, it can cool a bit when each ventures out to find what life is all about or when searching for a mate. It's during the late teens and early twenties that many twins fall away from each other, perhaps their relationship seems threatening to forming another healthy bond with a prospective husband or wife. The good news is that with time most twins find their way back to each other and resume a strong, healthy relationship, albeit a more mature one.

Society has always viewed multiples as naturally close regardless of zygosity or personality differences. Twins themselves often think that they should feel especially connected to their cotwin even when they may not. Two nontwin siblings whose personalities didn't mesh in their youth and who continue to live very separate adult lives wouldn't be looked at as an anomaly, but for twins who didn't care much for each other in their youth and continue a strained relationship as adults, the perception would be one of disbelief.

Twinning has also been tied up tightly with telepathy and extrasensory perception (ESP),

---

From One Parent to Another

"Alicia and Troy (DZOS) are best friends—they do everything together. It has never mattered that they are different sexes. They have always gotten along amazingly well and include one another in everything that they do."

---

even with the paranormal. Stories of one twin feeling the pain or anguish of a cotwin or knowing that imminent danger lurks just around the corner even when they were separated by thou-

---

From One Parent to Another

"I remember when Erica and Chris (DZOS) were born, I was especially concerned that they were unable to share a crib successfully. It seemed to me that by sleeping separately, they were missing out on some great cosmic bonding experience that all twins were supposed to share. I remember being at the post office one day with them when they were about four weeks old and running into an acquaintance there. As I juggled babies and mail, she commented on the logistical difficulties inherent in twins and asked whether I was planning on always bringing both with me when I did errands. 'Absolutely,' I responded. 'We're trying to keep them together as much as possible so that they can bond.' I still remember that encounter in the post office, but now I can't help but laugh at the naiveté of it. They're twins. They're going to be together so much the first few years of their lives that a trip to town isn't going to be the deal-maker or -breaker. They'll bond. No special effort is required!"

sands of miles make for great tabloid magazine covers. Yes, there are plenty of assumptions surrounding the twin bond, some true, some not so true.

In the Beginning

Since the beginning of time, there's been much speculation and mysticism surrounding twins. Many societies have revered twins and associated twinning with supernatural powers, while other cultures have viewed twinning as an evil omen and killed both the mother and the twins she bore. The theme of rivalry and dominance goes back thousands of years and appears in Greek mythology, where many gods were twins. Romulus and Remus, for instance, were set afloat on the Tiber River after their father, the Roman god Mars, abandoned them. They were raised by a she-wolf and became the mythological founders of Rome. Yet Romulus killed Remus in a struggle over power. Ah, yes, the first incident of twin rivalry! On the other hand, Gemini, the astrological twins, were inseparable and grew closer with age. So when one was killed during a battle, the other ended his own life to be with his brother. We read about twins in the Bible, too. In the Book of Genesis, for instance, Rebecca relates the struggle she felt her twins, Jacob and Esau, were having inside her—their rivalry and fight for dominance continued through their adulthood.

Until the advent of ultrasound technology, parents could only speculate on the intrauterine experience of twins. Today, because most women expecting multiples are classified as "high risk" by their doctors, parents have several opportunities to view how their multiples relate to each in utero through ultrasound. Not only is it an extraordinary sight to see two tiny babies side by side, but it's also a wonderful insight into their fetal behavior. Unfortunately, it's only possible to observe the pair up until approximately week twenty of gestation. After that, the babies are just too big to be viewed next to each other on the ultrasound monitor. So the question remains: Do multiples develop a connection at this early stage in their lives? Do they even sense the presence of their cotwin?

One way of gauging whether twins form a connection to each other during pregnancy—for better or worse—is when one loses his or her cotwin in utero. Since it's impossible to scientifically measure, the only evidence we have is the anecdotal expressions of loss related by the surviving twin. Yet does this sense of bereavement stem from the twin's own feelings, or from expressions of loss retold to the survivor over and over by her grieving parents until she accepted them as truth? Once again, it's impossible to know for sure. But one thing is for certain—a twin pregnancy with all its intratwin stimulation, not to mention tight quarters, is by far a very different environment than a singleton pregnancy.

Are Your Twins Telepathic?

Pick up any book about twins and more than likely you'll see something on telepathy, extrasensory perception, or the pair's ability to channel thoughts without the use of their cell phones. We want twins to have these paranormal abilities! It makes for fascinating cocktail chatter or at the very least confirms that twinship is indeed very special. There are three types of twin ESP: sympathetic pain, where one twin feels the "hurt" of the other twin regardless of their physical proximity; identical thought, where the pair think or say the exact same thing at the same time; and finally, imminent contact, where a twin knows she will see or hear from her cotwin within moments. With the risk of rocking the boat, though, there's no concrete scientific evidence to support twin telepathy. Twins, it seems, are no more telepathic than any other person walking the planet. Nonetheless, there are many twins who feel that they have a special, mystic connection to their cotwin and would insist that many multiples are indeed telepathic.

Several parents told me that they were certain their twins had a form of telepathy. These twins exhibited something more than just a mere coincidence, they said. For instance, one mom of MZm twins said she often finds her sons sleeping in the exact same positions yet in different beds, and when they were infants and she would nurse one, the other would move his mouth in a sucking motion even from across the room! It was as if he were being nursed at the same time. Another interesting tale comes from the mom who believes her daughters may be half-identical. One day she decided to teach her girls how to play Battleship, a game they had never seen before. Without consulting each other, the twins both laid out their ships in the exact same position, facing the same way (one was off by only one peg). There were several parents who said their twins knew when the other was hurt or when given the same written assignments produced nearly identical work. "I never felt that they communicated telepathically until this year when the teacher pulled me aside and told me they wrote almost the same essay but they were sitting across the room from each other," a mom of opposite-sex twins confided. "Since then I have been paying closer attention to work that comes home, and it is funny to see sometimes how they miss the same problem." Sometimes the twins' telepathy comes out in the form of artistic expression. More than one mom told me that her twins drew the same pictures while in different classrooms or sitting away from one another. Each child gave her creation the exact same title, too.

So why is it that some twins seem so in tune with one another? That they can finish their cotwin's sentences or know the instant their twin is hurting or in pain? The answer may be more associated with their genes (remember MZ twins share 100 percent of their DNA) and shared experiences than it does with the paranormal. Since identical twins have remarkably similar brain waves throughout their lives (we've all heard the expression "on the same wave length"), perhaps they do pick up each other's signals. Some researchers explain the telepathic hypothesis to twins' early understanding of each other's body language. Twins begin communicating with each other both preverbally and nonverbally very early in their lives. In fact, in one study of multiples who claimed to possess telepathic powers, researchers discovered that the subjects had cobedded with their cotwin during the first six months of their lives.

Having always looked for telepathy but never having seen any evidence, a mom of MZ girls instead reasoned, "They have a certain understanding of each other, but not to the point of being telepathic." Another mother whose MZ daughters often come down from separate bedrooms in the morning wearing the same outfit also shrugs off the telepathy theory and instead feels it stems from complete familiarity with each other.

NATURE VERSUS NURTURE: THE BIG DEBATE

What makes us who we are? Do our genetics or nature decide if we'll be Nobel Prize winners, artists, or teachers? Does our DNA determine if we'll abuse drugs or alcohol or live past the age of one hundred? Or is the environment in which we are raised, those nongenetic factors or nurture (where we live, our education, the values our parents instill in us, and so on), more indicative of how we'll behave or who we will end up being in life? Scientists have debated the question for decades, many focusing on comparing twins who were reared together and those who were reared apart as a way of gauging the influence

From One Parent to Another

"From the time they were born until the age of six, Nathaniel and Preston (MZm) were very close to the point of having their own language until the age of four. It was almost as if they were lost if the other wasn't around. At six, they began to explore the world around them and found it was fun to do things separately. That's also when the fighting and bickering started. My boys can really throw down, and to this day at the age of thirteen, they can really get into it. With all of that said they still have this unexplainable bond. They've tried to have separate bedrooms three times now. Each time they were separated, they would meet each other on the living room couch to fall asleep. So although it appears they want to be separate, they can't."

of genetics versus environment and their effect on personality development.

From 1979 through the 1990s, the Minnesota Study of Twins Reared Apart (MISTRA), for example, carefully evaluated more than one hundred sets of twins who were separated at birth, raised by different families, and then reunited as adults. (Many years ago, if twin babies were put up for adoption, they were often placed in different homes. Although this practice is unlikely today and seems somewhat cruel, it does allow scientists to study the nature-nurture aspect of twinship.) One of the largest and most detailed studies of its time, MISTRA's results indicate that nature is a strong force in determining an individual's personality.

On average, those MZ twins in the MISTRA study who were reared apart and then reunited as adults were just as similar in personality, tastes, and attitudes as MZ twins who had been reared together. The researchers concluded that psychological traits (such as IQ) are just as influenced by our genes as by our parents. In fact, a Swedish study found that eighty-year-old MZ twins are more cognitively alike than their younger twin counterparts, suggesting that even though these twins had more separate experiences as they aged, leading one to think they'd become more dissimilar, they actually became even more similar due to their genetic makeup, or nature.

But does nature and/or nurture have an effect on children during the early school years? Exactly when does it show up? A study conducted in 2001 in England showed that genetics did indeed have a strong influence on early school achievement, while shared twin environment had much less clout. Teachers assessed and rated seven-year-old participants who had completed their first year of primary school for a broad range of academic skills. All children were part of the Twins Early Development Study (or TEDS), a national, longitudinal study that examined more than fifteen thousand twins born in England and Wales from 1994 through 1996. The researchers found that identical (MZ) twin pairs scored a much higher correlation in reading, writing, and math skills than nonidentical (DZ) twins even when the MZ children were in different classrooms and rated by different teachers.

So does that mean that our children's destinies are preset and there's nothing we can do to help mold their futures? Of course not. A child's environment does play an important role: according to the researchers, the differences they did discover between MZ twins were due to the environment to which they were exposed. This can explain why so many twins seem to be polar opposites. It seems the more time some twins spend together, the more they unconsciously choose to be different. Yet if they were permanently separated, nature would take the driver's seat and steer each child toward choices, situations, and experiences that his or her innate essence finds pleasurable.

There are plenty of studies to lend support to the nurture theory as well. Just a few years ago, for instance, a study using participants from the TEDS program found that when same-sex twins were matched against their same-sex younger siblings during early childhood, the intratwin pairs had a substantially higher cognitive correlation. In other words, the twins were closer cognitively—both verbally and nonverbally—to each other than to their younger siblings. The correlation was very high for identical twins (MZ), since they share all of their DNA, but the correlation between nonidentical pairs (DZ) was also significantly higher compared with twin-to-sibling pairs. (Remember DZ twins and their nontwin siblings are genetically about the same.) So why do DZ twins have a higher cognitive similarity than their single-born siblings? There are many theories, but the best one is the "twin-specific shared environment" thesis. Because twins are the same age and develop along roughly the same time line, they share many of the same experiences at the same time. The study concluded that the nurture aspect of DZ twins' lives is more similar than that of their nontwin siblings.

The Impact of Shared and Nonshared Environments

Although the consensus is that genetics plays an important role in who we become, it doesn't mean that's the whole story. Environment—both shared and nonshared—does have a part, especially to those twins reared together.

A nonshared environment (experiences that are different for each multiple such as birth weight, classroom, sports, friends) can create differences between twins, while the shared environment (all that multiples have in common such as prenatal or in utero development, family life, even sharing the same classroom) explains the similarities between multiples that genetics simply can't.

Yet a shared environment can sometimes create differences in MZ twins or persuade one to think that nonidentical twins are more similar than perhaps they actually are. For instance, MZ twins are only "identical" in their genetic makeup. Although some MZ twins share one womb and one placenta (a shared environment), they may not receive identical amounts of nutrients, oxygen, or even blood. In short, their in utero experiences may be different. Fascinating, too, are the various ways in which MZ twins can be conceived—did the egg split immediately upon fertilization, each moving to an opposite side of the womb for implantation and each having its own placenta and sac, or did the fertilized egg begin to develop and then suddenly divide, both growing within the same sac? At first glance, it may appear that the latter group would enter the world most alike, but researchers speculate that may not be so. It's that second group that has to compete with each other for food, oxygen, and blood, leading to marked differences in their birth weight and size. What this means is simply that although MZ twins (and even MZ triplets) have the exact same genetic makeup, they come into this world as two very different individuals.

Case in point: due to prenatal differences, Jordan (MZm) was born with serious cardiac defects and required several surgeries in just the first few months of his life. According to his

> ### From One Parent to Another
>
> "Ryan and Christopher (zygosity unknown) have always been very close, best friends. They always have liked doing things together, and they really missed each other when they were apart. In the first grade, Ryan was home sick, and one of the teachers saw Christopher crying during recess. When she asked him what was the matter, he told her he missed his brother. In about fifth grade they started developing separate interests. Now one takes drum lessons, the other takes guitar. In the last year, they do not like to look like each other or be confused for their brother. They want different haircuts so that they look less alike."

mom, he and his twin Gabriel have always had a big physical distinction between them even though they're genetically identical. Now at nine years of age, Gabriel is still slightly bigger. The boys differ cognitively, too.

Furthermore, a shared environment (family life, same class-room, and so forth) may not affect MZ twins in exactly the same way as each individual perceives and reacts to every event uniquely—one may see the glass half full while the other sees the glass half empty.

Shared and nonshared environments have a different effect on DZ twins, too. Although nonidentical twins have approximately only 50 percent of their genes in common, making them no more alike genetically than single siblings, DZ twins may have had very similar or parallel in utero experiences, receiving equal amounts of blood and nutrients. During the first year of life, both develop at the approximate same time, taking their first steps or speaking their first words within months (and sometimes days) of each other. The result is that while DZ twins may enter the world more alike than their MZ counterparts, with time, genetics will take over making MZ twins more similar (Jordan is bound to catch up to his brother Gabriel in the coming years), while DZ twins will grow and change and undoubtedly become very different individuals both physically and cognitively.

My own nonidentical boys are a perfect example of this. Both born bald and weighing six pounds twelve ounces and six pounds eight ounces respectively—a mere four-ounce differ-ence—we could hardly tell them apart for the first few months. They uttered their first words and began to walk within days of each other. Strangers often assumed they were identical. Yet here we are ten years later, and one is nearly two inches taller than the other. They look and act so differently now that most people hardly recognize that they are in fact twins.

Dealing with Disabilities

The chances of having a multiple with a disability such as learning problems or cerebral palsy are higher than with a singleton child (statistically cerebral palsy is six times greater with twins, thirty times greater with triplets). MZ twins have an even higher incidence of being born with a disability than nonidentical twins.

Parents' response upon hearing the news that one twin is impaired is usually that of bereavement, fear, guilt, and sometimes even anger as the healthy cotwin is often a reminder—a mirror image of what the disabled twin could have been. Some parents even mourn the loss of a normal twinship between the siblings.

The healthy twin deals with issues of his own. He may hold himself back to draw less attention to his struggling cotwin. He may feel guilt ("Why did I survive unimpaired?") and even jealousy because the disabled twin receives additional attention from health-care professionals, family, and friends. He may even try to care for the disabled twin to ease his guilt. On the surface this behavior may appear to be noble, caring, and compassionate, but his good deeds can go too far and become all too consuming for a young child.

Still, there are many positive aspects to this type of twinship. Most healthy twins with a disabled cotwin become sensitive adults. Their view of the world is not so self-centered, and they are often more respectful of others with disabilities—many go on to become health-care professionals as adults. And finally, many develop a deep sense of self-confidence that comes from helping out whenever they can.

However, there are a few parameters that parents need to consider when they have one twin who is healthy and one who is disabled.

- Explain often and from the beginning to the healthy twin about the situation with his cotwin. Make sure he understands that the condi-

(continued on next page)

tion is not his fault in any way. Many healthy twins who didn't understand and were kept in the dark until later in life spent their young lives confused and hurt by what they thought was special treatment toward the cotwin. Twins who understand the situation from the beginning and are able to confidently articulate the circumstances to others usually grow up very accepting of the disability rather than resentful and often find balance within their relationship.

- Don't shy away from the same after-school sport for each for fear of highlighting the gap in abilities. As a mother of a disabled DZ triplet told me, "Competition has helped with Matt's disability." Without the unspoken competition from his siblings, she explained, her son might not have pushed himself as hard physically.
- The disabled child may be sensitive to what looks like exaggerated praise for simple tasks. Parents and teachers need to adequately commend as well as discipline the disabled child, too.
- Parents with a disabled child greatly need and benefit from outside help so that they can devote time and often much-needed attention to the healthy twin, too.
- Rather than excluding him, allow the healthy twin to join in some of the therapy sessions.

THE TWIN ADVANTAGE: THE REAL STORY

Twins may not have the ability to read each other's minds and use this superpower for good, not evil, but there are other tangible benefits to being a twin. They develop a deep trust in each other. Multiples often draw strength from each other during times of stress and sorrow. From the very beginning they cultivate an emotional and social support system that offers a solid base that they will draw on again and again throughout their lives. (Take the sad and strange case back in the 1970s of twins who were locked in a basement for six years by their step-mother. Due to their twinship, each offered the other mental stimulation that prevented permanent damage.)

By the time twins reach the school years, they are just as emotionally ready as their singleton classmates to take on the task of learning. In fact, some multiples may be more secure stemming from the strong relationship they already have with their cotwin. Due to their unique situation, they learn early on the art of negotiation, compromise, and sharing. A cotwin's physical presence isn't always necessary—the bond between them is often enough to sustain the two even if they're apart for part of the day. (Although for twins who are tightly bonded, separation may need to happen more gradually.)

And while some children lack a strong relationship with their father, twins usually have a much earlier association with their dads. After all, Dad had to help with the feeding and diapering during their infancy. In the process he built an early bond that continues as the twins grow and develop. Children who have strong relationships with both their mother and their father will ultimately feel more emotionally secure, helping them to successfully journey through other relationships.

Twins are often very protective of each other, each acting as a personal bodyguard for the other. Playground bullies are less likely to mess with one twin when they know that their "victim" has a strong ally who would fight to the finish for her. Most parents tell their kids they should stick up for each other when they see that one is in trouble on the playground. Most twins know this instinctively. One mom told me that her non-identical daughters always had separate lives even from early childhood, but yet one day when one twin was in trouble on the preschool playground, her cotwin came running from clear across the asphalt to lay out her sister's bully!

From One Parent to Another

"At age ten, soon to be eleven, Joseph and Jack (MZm) are competitive. They want to outdo each other. They fight and get on each other's nerves at times. They also tease each other quite a bit, and there's name calling. I find it really funny when one calls the other ugly because they are identical. But sometimes after the fighting, especially at night, I will go into their room (they share one), and there they are both sacked out in the same bunk."

And what about those tenuous teen years? Having a buddy for moral support throughout a host of new social situations is a blessing. No awkward moments standing at the side of the gymnasium all alone during the school dance. With your cotwin by your side (or at least within your sight line), you feel at ease and relaxed. The pressures of high school academics, getting ready for college and leaving home, the ups and downs of dating are alleviated thanks to the twinship. This is extra important during the tumultuous teen years when every comment or look can have hundreds of different meanings.

And finally, it's the twins themselves who show us time and time again the positive impact of their twinship—friendship, a constant companion through thick and thin. Most twins continue this close relationship into their adult years. Their early friendship gives way to a mature confidant—someone who understands and is going through the same life trials.

And dare I mention that twins tend to be more popular in school? Whether it's the twin status that intrigues others to want to get to know them or the fact that the twin partnership itself allows twins to feel more secure, thus attracting others to them, most older twins report having many friends and positive experiences during the school years. In fact, studies have shown that opposite-sex adolescent twins have an easier time interacting with peers since they have more opportunities. The nature of their birth status gives them greater access to practice positive interaction with opposite-sex peers. These twins actually benefit socially due to their sibling bond.

Multiples as Adults

Will your twins or triplets be close when they're adults? While some multiples may rejoice when they hit the college years, finally free from the confines of twin bondage, most will remain close, if not in proximity at least in spirit. So what does the future hold in store for your multiples? Some of it depends on their zygosity or twin type—identical twins with their shared genetic makeup usually lead the pack in retaining a strong, close-knit bond, followed by same-sex fraternal twins. Twins' relationship through childhood and how they cope with the tumultuous teen years will also determine what kind of friends they'll be once they become adults. Many twin siblings band together during adolescence, taking comfort in having a same-age confidant, but if their peer group—that omnipotent entity—doesn't appreciate their twinship and encourages one to reject the other, it could push the pair apart.

Research shows that overall, twins marry later in life than singletons, probably due to the twins' deep bond and friendship. If you have a twin partnership that complements you in nearly every way, there's no need or hurry to find a soul mate. Perhaps, too, twins feel reluctant to form another pairing since they already have an established successful relationship. Or maybe leaving the twinship feels like a betrayal to some. This can be seen as both a blessing and a curse. On the one hand, it's wise to be choosy when it comes to picking a lifelong partner as statistics show that marrying later in life helps its odds of longevity. Conversely some multiples may hide behind their union, fearing that they may not be able to make it on their

From One Parent to Another

"I told both Sheila and Virginia (DZSSf) from the beginning that this is going to be your best friend when you grow up so save time and be each other's best friend now. Now in college they don't see each other or communicate with each other that much. They keep up through us. We went to visit Virginia at the university, and Sheila's marching band just happened to be in town for a competition. We didn't tell Virginia that Sheila was going to be there. When they saw each other, there were huge hugs and tears. It was very emotional."

own. In the end, it's the multiples who were accepting of their cotwin's outside friendships during childhood who find it easier to welcome a new partnership for their cotwin in adulthood. Often when one twin marries, the second seems to find a marriage partner shortly thereafter, the former having paved the way for the latter to jump in.

Sometimes when singletons marry a twin, they may not fully understand the close relationship that twins share. In rare cases, when nontwin spouses feel that they come second in the marriage and the twinship comes first, the nontwin spouse may try to break up the union or, at the very least, limit contact between the pair. Maybe this explains why some twins marry other twins. This would make sense in that each understands the twin alliance and the subtle nuances that accompany it. When one set of identical twins marries another set of identical twins, it's called a quaternary marriage. It's rare, to be sure, probably fewer than three hundred couples worldwide, but it does happen. Stranger still are these two couples' children—not only are the offspring first cousins, but they are full genetic siblings too since their identical parents share 100 percent of their DNA.

The most intriguing statistics about adult twins, however, comes from the Minnesota Twin Study. Researchers there wanted to know how genes affect our love lives. They postulated that since MZ twins share the exact same DNA, they would also have the same criteria for a mate. (If one twin has a penchant for blondes, then his cotwin will too.) Furthermore, they speculated, MZ twins would be attracted to their cotwins' spouses. ("My brother has great taste in women!") Makes sense, especially when you consider the quaternary marriages discussed above. Yet when they tested their theory, it crumbled right before their eyes! Not only were the spouses of the MZ twins no more alike than any other partners of random people, but also the male MZ twins felt no attraction for their brothers' wives. In fact, two-thirds felt indifference or downright dislike for them. The researchers' conclusion? Love has no rhyme or reason; it's completely unpredictable and random.

> ## From One Parent to Another
>
> "The closeness of Dan and Todd's (DZSSm) relationship has always had an ebb and flow to it. At the foundation is a natural love and admiration for each other, but their connection is sometimes stretched thin by other demands on their time and by their outside friendships and interests. I think that now, as they have grown into young men in college, they have a new appreciation for each other; but I also see a desire to break away, not only from each other, but from the family in general as each makes his own way in life."

In adulthood many twins actually grow closer to one another, developing a deeper friendship than they had during childhood. As each twin develops his or her separate life, the rivalry and comparisons that were so evident during adolescence finally wither and die. With the twin pressure no longer an issue, the two are finally free to thoroughly enjoy their special relationship.

And finally, researchers concluded that a tight emotional bond between adult MZ twins actually increases their life span (there was no correlation in life span between DZ twins). A study found that MZ twins who spoke to each other at least once a month via telephone or in person lived longer on average than those who didn't.

A FRIEND FOR LIFE

And so we come full circle—born together, twins become instant companions and playmates and develop a high-access relationship that will affect them socially and psychologically more than that of two single-born siblings. As they mature, they may drift from each other or veer off onto separate roads as they try to figure out who they are as individuals and what they want from life. This is only natural and shouldn't be discouraged, although it may be much harder for one cotwin than the other. But the strength of your multiples' early bond will often sustain the pair through this period of growth, and once the pressure of adolescence is behind them, most multiples come home to each other to once again enjoy their special union.

2

Developing Identity and Promoting Individuality

As a single-born person, I've taken my individuality for granted. When I look in the mirror, I see myself. There's no one else like me. Yet for some multiples, especially for those who look exactly alike, finding out who they are sometimes isn't so easy.

Many different factors affect twins' identity and individuality—parents' and families' attitudes, the culture in which they live, and how the twins themselves view their relationship. If parents, for instance, value unity and familial solidarity over independence and encourage their multiples to work together and rely on each other, the twins themselves will most likely adopt the same way of thinking.

When it comes to multiples and individuality, it's all about balance—learning to nurture their special bond while at the same time giving them the freedom to discover and explore their own distinct worlds. When a twin enjoys a healthy view of himself, it actually strengthens the intratwin relationship—without the pressure of battling to be seen as different from one's cotwin, there's actually more opportunity to enjoy their bond.

IDENTITY CHALLENGES FOR TWINS AND MULTIPLES

Within the first few weeks of life, newborns quickly develop a dependent relationship—a union—with their mother. To babies, the borders between themselves and their caregiver are blurred. They believe the two are one and the same. Slowly as they grow and become more mobile, however, they begin to discover there's a world outside of this relationship. They realize that they are separate—both physically and psychologically—from their mother as well as from their environment. It's around the ages of five to thirty-six months that all children, multiples included, begin this slow process of separation and individuation as they detach from the mother-child relationship and their own personalities take shape. Although not consciously, they begin to ask the ultimate question, "Who am I?" Completing this two-step process is vital to developing autonomy—every child needs to establish a clear sense of self, to act independently, and to form strong relationships with others.

Since twins come into the world as a couple, they identify not only with their mother but with their cotwin as well. Therefore, the separation-individuation phase can be a bit more complicated. Twins realize they are separate from their mother much sooner than they understand they are also separate from each other. Perhaps it's because most infant multiples are nearly inseparable and therefore don't have the same opportunities for self-discovery as single-born babies. Mom may get a babysitter or enroll her children in day care and go off for an hour or to work for the whole day, for instance, but one's cotwin is still there. Twins and other multiples eat together, sleep together, bathe together, and play together. In short, in infancy and early childhood they spend much more time with each other than they do with their mother, and that may delay their separation.

Mom may unwittingly aggravate the process as well. Shortly after giving birth, she may relate to them as a pair since it's difficult for one woman to emotionally invest in two infants at once. And even when Mom successfully attaches to each individually, the world at large may continue to pressure her to see them as a single entity with comments such as, "How can you tell them apart? They look so much alike!"

Furthermore, on most days, Mom's attention is split between the pair. When a twin does have a moment of her time for a cuddle or a hug, his or her cotwin is always there waiting for a turn. Studies have shown that mothers of multiples have more interrupted interaction with their children than mothers of singletons. (But you already knew that, didn't you?) Twins spend much less time physically alone with their mother, too, a crucial component to developing autonomy—it's Mom's exclusive emotional support that makes a child feel secure and in turn helps drive her child's quest for individuation.

It can be a double-edged sword—as twins take great pleasure in their relationship, compensating in part for their lack of individual maternal attention, they may jeopardize their own personal individuation in the process. The result, although rare, may be low self-esteem, trouble acting independently, and frustration in obtaining and maintaining outside relationships later in their lives. Identity is also tied up with cognitive development since it takes an emotional maturity to problem solve. (It's important to stress here that most twins will develop a strong sense of self—even if some are delayed in this process—and go on to lead normal, fulfilling lives.)

From One Parent to Another

"Elise (MZf) decided in sixth grade to play clarinet in the school band. It took some courage because Suzanne (MZf) had no interest in that and so Elise did it on her own. Suzanne has been taking art lessons without Elise for a year and a half and loving it. We support both of these decisions and respect them for it. Suzanne also cut off thirteen inches of her hair last year for Locks of Love. It was a major act of separation because it was suddenly very easy to tell who was who. Elise decided not to do that, and we supported that as well."

Twin Subgroups: Do They Develop Their Identity Differently?

Developing individual identity is a different experience for everyone. Many psychologists have examined the issue over the years. For instance, psychologist Sara Smilansky, a professor of child clinical and educational psychology, studied how Israeli twins develop their own identities. Using a series of tests and interviews with the twins, Smilansky devised a system—an individuation score—to determine a child's self-awareness and level of autonomy. The questionnaire addresses twins' self-perceptions by rating their feelings on their intrapair relationships, their likes, dislikes, moods, reactions, and so forth. In her research, Smilansky found that while single-born children in grades two to four were already strongly individualized, nonidentical (DZ) twins were not nearly as much, with opposite-sex twins faring better with individuation than same-sex fraternal twins. Identical (MZ) twins were the least individuated at this age. Looking ahead to fifth and sixth grade, DZ twins were still behind singletons but not as much as in grades two to four (opposite-sex twins once again had higher individuation scores than same-sex fraternal twins), but there was little change in the MZ group. They had not made any significant progress toward individuating during the three-year time span.

Furthermore, a longitudinal Swedish study that followed a group of twins for sixteen years obtained similar findings. Using the Wartegg Drawing Test to determine a twin child's self-confidence, self-esteem, levels of anxiety and aggression, how the child handled conflict, and so on—all components that make up a child's identity—researchers concluded that out of the different subgroups of multiples, DZ twins possessed the strongest sense of self, both same-sex and opposite-sex pairs. Once again, MZ twins had the hardest time individuating, with MZ girls demonstrating more reliance on their cotwins and less on their parents than DZ girls.

So why is it that out of the

> **From One Parent to Another**
>
> "I had read about twins not recognizing their own reflection in a mirror, so we worked at trying to establish their individual identities from early on. We would play peek-a-boo in a mirror saying, "Where is Kaden? (MZm) There he is!" by moving back and forth in the view of a mirror. Then we would do the same thing showing both boys together. Even so, they still had trouble with 'we' statements. It was always, "Can we . . . ?" even if only one of them was asking. We had to work our way from 'we,' to 'me,' then finally 'I.' This wasn't firmly established until just before they started kindergarten."

six subgroups, MZ twins have the hardest time developing individual identity? There are many components contributing to delayed autonomy that affect all twins, but identical children face additional hurdles. First, developing simultaneously with one's cotwin can be confusing at times, clouding each child's self-awareness. When an identical twin looks in the mirror, she often recognizes the face of her cotwin rather than herself. In fact, research shows that MZ twin babies often take up to six months longer to identify themselves in a mirror than DZ twins. Even older, adolescent MZ twins often make mistakes when gazing in a mirror. Many twins report feeling confused when seeing a mirror image, not realizing at first exactly who's staring back. Many young twins also answer to the name of their cotwin as well as their own, sometimes calling themselves by the name of their cotwin. It's no wonder really when neighbors, teachers, and even parents continue to call the twins by the wrong name or relate to both as one person. The twins themselves may doubt exactly who they are. (In one study where a large group of children including a set of twins played together, the other classmates consistently treated the multiples as one.) Furthermore, it's when children play with others that are different in personality, ability, and experiences that their own sense of identity grows. Some MZ twins prefer to play with just each other and will not experience these benefits of socializing with others.

Don't Overlook the Dual Identity

Although you've just read several pages on the problems that some multiples may encounter in developing a sense of self, delayed autonomy is not necessarily inevitable. Furthermore, parents shouldn't dismiss their multiples' dual identity in the hopes of promoting their individuality. Twins have their own individual identity, but they also have their identity as a multiple, a pair, that should not be dismissed. And while it's important for each child to develop his or her own strengths outside of the shadow of a cotwin, it's equally important to acknowledge the special bond and union of the twinship. The mission of parents should therefore be to encourage their twins—and all their children—to follow the beat of their own drums.

On the other hand, in a parent's haste to have each twin form his own individuality, he or she may push the issue a bit too far. For instance, if you believe that your twins would benefit from being in separate classrooms, it may not be necessary to separate them at home by giving each his own bedroom. Never force a separation on your twins since it can have the opposite effect of what was intended. Instead of feeling more independent, your twins may feel defensive and anxious and cling to each other even more.

Should You Worry?

For many multiples developing a strong, personal sense of self may never become a problem. Yes, it may take longer than if a twin were born a singleton, but it happens nonetheless. Yet if a twin is still having difficulties by the time she reaches secondary school, it may be because she feels that she works better as a team than solo. A parent's positive attitude, illuminating the beneficial possibilities waiting for discovery, can help. As you gently assist your multiples in developing a sense of autonomy, you may find it easier to think of this period of individuation as rebalancing their relationship rather than separating or breaking up the pair, which has negative connotations.

Several parents of identical twins that I interviewed were very cognizant of their children establishing a strong sense of

---

From One Parent to Another

"Once when they (MZm) were about two and a half years old and we were at my mom's house, they were playing hide-and-seek in her closet that had mirrors on it. One boy was hiding in the closet and laughing. His brother heard him and went to find him. When he saw himself in the mirror, he reached out to grab his brother. He had a really funny look when he realized it wasn't his brother. They played in that closet and with the mirror for more than an hour. One boy would get into the closet and the other would close the door and look at himself, then they would change places. At one point, they both stood outside the closet, closed the door, and touched their reflections in the mirror. I think this is when they first realized that they looked alike. It was really neat to watch them as they learned through their playing."

From One Parent to Another

"We offer Gabriel and Jordan (MZm) options—would you like to go to this camp or that camp? Would you like to take this class or that class? If they choose the same one, that's fine; and if they choose a different one, that's fine, too. A lot of times they choose to do the same thing, but sometimes they specifically want something different from each other."

self from a young age. Many told me that they stressed using each child's name rather than calling them collectively "the twins." They encouraged their children to think and speak for themselves, too.

PROMOTING INDIVIDUALITY

It's a delicate balance promoting multiples' individuality while nurturing their liaison. On one hand, we all understand how special and deep-rooted the relationship is between our multiples. Yet as a society, we value those who are unique, independent, and strong, a maverick that stands out in the crowd. And the twins, triplets, and quads want to be seen as individuals themselves, even though for some it's harder to articulate than it is for others. So is it possible to do both at the same time? Absolutely. When you promote individuality between your twins, you'll actually help them to deepen their intratwin relationship. It may seem counterintuitive, but when multiples are allowed to develop their own tastes, interests, and personalities, it takes the pressure off of the rivalry and permits twins more opportunity to enjoy the "we" part of their relationship instead of fighting to express the "I."

You don't have to force your young twins to spend hours apart as babies to help them develop a sense of self either. As every parent of multiples knows, that would be a huge imposition! From sheer practicality, twins need to do certain things together such as bathing and eating so that their parents have a

---

From One Parent to Another

"I always let Natalie and Abigail (DZSSf) pick out their after-school activities. They do play the same activities, but I encourage the coaches and instructors to separate them. Whenever I can, I will sign them up on different days, too, or on different teams."

---

moment to rest. Instead try a simple one-on-one outing an hour a week from the time they're very little to get the ball rolling.

In addition, there are many little things parents can do within the home when multiples are very young that can help the individualizing process. For instance, have your babies nap at different times so you can coo with the child who's awake or let each parent take a child into a different room and play or read one-on-one. But most important is parental perception and behavior—children look to their parents for guidance, for their reactions, and if Mom or Dad continues to view and treat their twins as a pair, the twins will view themselves that way as well. In all that you say and do, relate to each one individually. Although it's never too late to help twins develop autonomy, it's important to begin the process early in a multiple's life since children are more strongly influenced by parents when they are young.

What Parents Can Do

When you take steps to ensure that each child develops a sense of self very early in your multiples' lives, it will help lay the groundwork for healthy future attitudes and relationships not only with those around them but with each other as well. Here are a few other strategies to adopt.

From One Parent to Another

"I realized very early on that Rick and James (MZm) did better together if they had some time apart during the day. It didn't matter what they did that was separate from each other, just that they had some down time alone. I think giving them time to be individuals was as important as them getting along and bonding. They would always be there for each other no matter how they fought—if someone else got out of line, they would defend each other. I used lots of sports and crafts; both lend themselves to the group as well as the individual."

- Starting from an early age (or as soon as is practical), allow each child to have her own belongings—don't group all toys, favorite books, or clothing together. Give individual ownership instead. It's fine for twins to share clothes (it sure is easier), but allow each child to have a few favorites of her very own. (As they get older, allow them to decide for themselves how much clothes sharing will go on. After all, one of the benefits to having a female, teenage cotwin is having double the wardrobe!) Give each child a special treasure box or small bookcase for stashing personal trinkets.

- Although photographs of the duo are precious, take plenty of solo pictures of each of your multiples as they grow and change as well. Create a separate album, memory book, or memento box for each rather than just having one for "the twins."

- Acknowledge their individual likes and dislikes from the food they eat and the clothing they wear to their favorite colors and cartoon characters. Some parents even let each twin decorate her side of the shared bedroom any way she

---

From One Parent to Another

"Because my triplets are fraternal, they look different from each other. But I was always concerned about treating them like a group, rather than as individuals, because I did everything together with all three. It was a logistic issue for me, and I felt that it was important to treat them equally and fairly. Only I worried that by doing so, I would be suppressing their individuality. I didn't have the luxury of time or money to take only one somewhere with me at a time, but I did, and still do, try to make quiet time, or individual time, with them at home. I take turns teaching them how to cook, working with them on homework, or playing a game."

---

chooses. From early on, nurture individual creative expression, qualities, and talents, whether in music, art, or even writing. Some twins who have a harder time in seeing their uniqueness will need parental guidance.

- Make it a priority to spend time alone with each young twin every day. Introduce gradual, planned separation outside the home, too. Begin with a short period of separation when your twins are very young, and increase the duration as they age. The older children who have the most difficulty with separation are the ones who never experienced time alone when they were young, but it's never too late to start. The goal is for each multiple to feel that time apart from one's cotwin is normal and natural, that it's OK to be on your own. Be sensitive to times when they truly want to be together and be flexible—never force the issue. Think creatively: one mom told me that logistically it's just too difficult to take her boy-girl twins out individually. Instead, she said, one parent often goes outside to play baseball or badminton with one twin while the other parent stays inside and hangs out with the other.

- Assign each twin a different household chore—one sets the table, the other folds the laundry—allowing each to develop the confidence to work independently.

Birthday Party Basics

With all this talk about promoting individuality, there is one thing that twins have to share—a birthday. Many parents told me ways in which they made the party special for each of their multiples. For instance, one mom of teenage daughters had back-to-back slumber parties— one daughter invited friends for Friday night, the other daughter had girlfriends sleep over Saturday night. While a smashing success, she doesn't recommend it. "It was a long weekend," she said. This year, she revamped her idea: everyone slept over the same night, but when it was time for bed, each twin retired to her own bedroom with her own special group of friends.

Since my sons' birthday fell during the winter Olympics this year, we used that theme to create the perfect parallel party—two teams of Olympiads competing for the gold. Each boy was the captain of a squad consisting of his personally invited guests, giving at least the illusion of two separate parties.

There are many other ways to make each child feel like she's the sole center of attention on her special day. Here are a few other ideas to help you shine the spotlight on each of your multiples.

- It's just as easy to buy or bake two small cakes as it is to buy or bake one big one. And don't forget to sing Happy Birthday twice, taking turns who goes first each year. (In our house, we alternate years, one taking the even years, the other the odd.)
- Obviously it's recommended that gifts be different based on each child's personal wish list. Yet what happens if they both want an

expensive dollhouse? Sharing large, big-ticket items is fine; just top it off with a small, personalized toy for each.

- Consider splitting up the guest list and having your multiples send out separate invitations (maybe separate designs of each child's choosing). This not only allows each child to have a personal stake in the party, but it also doesn't obligate the recipient to bring two presents when he or she may in fact be friendly with only one twin.
- For opposite-sex twins where a common theme may be more difficult, try a smaller party for each child on different days with just a few choice friends. As they reach the teen years and interest in the opposite sex grows, you'll be able to once again successfully combine parties (and from what I hear from parents, their opposite-sex twins loved those events).

Making It Easy for Outsiders

Contrary to what it may seem like on days when you get silly comments from strangers ("How do you ever tell them apart?"), most single-born people would like to treat multiples as individuals, but they often need some extra help in identifying each child. In other words, if you make it easy for people to view your multiples as unique beings, they probably will. If your multiples are opposite-sex or fraternal twins that look nothing alike, that's a huge help, but it's not the whole solution. Without a way to identify each child (especially for identical twins and triplets), most teachers, neighbors, and even relatives will avoid getting to know your twins separately for fear of making a mistake. They'll avoid using their names, for instance, often keeping the conversation superficial, or worse,

From One Parent to Another

"When Victoria (MZf) turned three, she took it upon herself to stake out her own identity. She and Kate (MZf) were beginning preschool at a local church cooperative, and one day she came down dressed and ready for school wearing a coonskin cap with her preschool dress. We just looked at her dumbfounded and thought, 'What a cute little sense of style!' It wasn't just a one-day occurrence—she wore that coonskin cap everywhere for well over a year. And so from the time she was three, Victoria has had a little more desire to identify herself—in a good way—and to help others to immediately know who each of them were."

steering clear of it altogether. Kids are sensitive to this, too, when for instance the teacher greets everyone by name in the morning but not the twins for fear that she may call them by the wrong names.

Identical Dress and Older Twins

At some point in their lives, you've probably dressed your children alike (or at least similarly). And why not? You're proud of your multiples and want the world to know how special they are. While the practice may seem completely innocent and just fun, parents need to recognize that it's not often in the best interest of their kids. Dressing them alike once in a while won't have long-term negative effects. But is there a problem with dressing multiples identically on a consistent basis? Yes. First of all, carbon-copy clothing can blur reality and subtly implies to the public that multiples are one and the same, not the single people they actually are. And for MZ twins who look and dress exactly alike, the task to tell them apart is that much greater, thereby muddling an outsider's ability to treat them as individuals. Plus, once the practice of dressing alike starts, it's difficult to stop.

Dressing alike has consequences for the multiples themselves, too. Clothing choice is a strong component for identity formation as it's an outward presentation of ourselves and it contributes to an internal sense of who we are. For those children who have always dressed alike, the practice can become an integral part of their twinship. Dressing identically reinforces their dual identity, confounding the process of developing autonomy. And by holding steadfastly to this twin tradition, many twins begin to believe subconsciously that they are unable to make it on their own.

Not surprisingly, identical twin girls dress alike more often than fraternal girls or either type of male multiples. The consequence for MZ girls who continue to dress alike regularly as they reach preadolescence may give some parents a reason to discourage the practice. Identical girls sometimes have a harder time developing their own positive visual body image since they view themselves through their same-dressed cotwin. They simply have a harder time internally visualizing themselves—there's no need to since their cotwin acts as a mirror doing it for them.

> ### From One Parent to Another
>
> "I have always stressed individuality. From the time Joshua and Anthony (MZm) were a few months old, I stopped dressing them alike. If someone gave us identical outfits, both outfits went into one son's dresser drawer. I preferred similar outfits of either different colors or different designs. They each have always had their own birthday cake and no shared presents. When someone gives one present for both of them to share (like at Christmas or birthdays), I find out what it is and make sure it is something that can really be shared, and if not, I either give it to only one boy, go get another item similar so they both have a present, or put it into my 'regift box' and use it at a party they are invited to."

What Parents Can Do

Parents have a strong role in helping to establish their multiples' social identity. You can assist others to see the special and unique qualities of each of your children and try to promote to your multiples that life is filled with personal choices and many different exciting possibilities.

- Teach your multiples, especially MZ children, to introduce themselves by name. This will help outsiders not only identify them more easily, but it will help put the outsiders more at ease, allowing them to truly get to know each multiple for himself. If, for instance, teachers and classmates are having trouble distinguishing one from the other, teach your children to give them clues: "I'm the one with the freckle on my left cheek," or "I'm a lefty while she's right-handed."
- Explain to your children that identical dress does not make the twin bond, and conversely, dressing differently doesn't break it. If your twins object to dressing dissimilarly, realize that they have no experience with it and the unknown is

---

From One Parent to Another

"Whenever people would call them 'the twins,' we'd say, 'Their names are Ashleigh and Amanda (DZSSf).' We also encouraged the girls to go by their names. This was a little harder for them to get used to when they were younger. They'd always want to introduce themselves as Ashleigh-Amanda (said all together), since that's how it sounded to them. During the first couple of years of their lives, my husband and I took studio pictures with each girl separately so that they'd have pictures of just themselves with Mommy and Daddy for when they grew up. I'm a big scrapbooker, too, and all of my children have their own baby album, school album, and sports album."

always scary. They may lack the confidence to be different. Or some may feel that they are betraying the twinship if they dress differently. Stress that even when they dress differently they are still twins. Until they're more comfortable, though, you can help them make the transition to dressing differently by suggesting a variation on their clothing motif—same clothes, different colors or same pants, different tops and shoes.

- If your children need to wear uniforms to school, encourage them to accessorize differently—dissimilar hair bands, jewelry, shoes, and even different backpacks.
- Experiment with different hairstyles until each child finds that one that feels right to her.

Just Mommy and Me

Spending time alone with each multiple is important on many fronts—it allows each the chance to have solo time with Mom or Dad, to express himself honestly without the fear of being overheard or even judged by a cotwin, and an opportunity to slowly wean himself from his cotwin. Parents also benefit by getting to know their twins individually and developing a deeper bond with each child singularly rather than as part of a unit. It's fascinating and a bit startling at first when you realize that the pair personality of your twins is very different from the individual character of each.

The parents who found a way to carve out time alone with each multiple discovered it was enormously pleasurable and beneficial to the parent-child relationship. One mom told me she loves doing hotel sleepovers, complete with in-room movies and dinners out with each of her daughters. "It's nice to just have one child with you from time to time," she said. "They are able to talk to you without interruptions from a sibling, and I find now that the girls are preteen, that this is when they

(continued on next page)

Just Mommy and Me *(continued)*

really open up to me since they often don't want to open up in front of a sibling." Another mom remembers the time spent alone with each child, whether going to the video arcade with her son or going to nice restaurants with her daughter, as the most memorable of their childhoods. Parents were practical in their approach, too: to help keep track of her "dates" with each of her daughters, one mom of triplets color-coded the days on a calendar to be certain of whose turn it was. One dad took advantage of his flextime at work and alternated afternoons out with each of his twins.

Yet sometimes separating young twins can be a slippery slope. It can be scary for some if it's the first time they've ever spent time away from their cotwin or if it's the first time they've had to interact with a parent solo. (That's why it's important to start the ritual when they're babies and less aware.) This is another great reason to spend time alone with each child—twins need to develop that individual personality, the ability to think and act independently. If this is all new for you and your multiples, here are a few tips to help it get off to a smashing start.

- If your multiples have never spent any time apart, start out with short trips (a fifteen-minute jaunt to the bank and post office, for instance) and then gradually build up the time away as they get older and more comfortable. Now that my kids are older, I always take one out for an entire weekend morning to run errands and then top it off with something he would like to do such as hitting the video game store or stopping by his favorite fast-food spot.
- Keep careful tabs on whose turn it is to go with Mom or Dad. (Multiples can get very sensitive if you inadvertently skip their turn.) And don't forget the single-sibling triad as well. Try taking one multiple with his single-born sibling out for a day, too—it helps to build a

Just Mommy and Me *(continued)*

bond between a twin with his older or younger sibling, a relationship that's often overlooked.

- Don't let guilt for not spending enough alone time with each one make you overcompensate—there's no need to talk the poor child's ear off or indulge him in every sugary wish. A child takes comfort and pleasure in just knowing that his mother or father is there with only him, so relax.

- If spending time alone with each child proves difficult, on occasion a relative or close friend can step in to aptly act as a temporary surrogate parent or confidant. After all, you not only want to build the parent-child relationship, but you also want each twin to feel comfortable without the other.

From One Parent to Another

"I started taking my boys out separately in preschool. Andrew and Jeffrey (DZSSm) were in the three-year-old class and Joey was in the four-year-old class. On Fridays I would keep one of them home with me and the other two would go to preschool. We'd go to breakfast or shopping and to lunch—whatever we needed to do between the time of preschool starting and preschool ending. It was just the two of us. I loved it and the kids looked forward to it, too."

MULTIPLES AND FRIENDSHIPS

Among twin researchers, one of the more hotly debated topics centers on friendship, namely, does being a twin help or hinder formation of peer friendships? Those who agree with the former say that a twin's strong emotional base with his cotwin would actually make him feel more secure in venturing out to find new friends. To a certain degree, that's true. Female twins, for instance, often use their twinship to promote themselves socially. Many children see the couple as celebrities and are naturally drawn to play with them. Yet with the exception of middle and high school twins, where twinship has been shown to be an asset in peer formation, most of the research today supports the latter theory—young twins (preschool and early elementary school) have less diversity in their friendships and are socially more withdrawn than single-born children.

To understand why, let's look at the typical life of a young set of twins. Since most households with multiples are very busy, parents often find it a chore to arrange outside play dates, and since their twins have built-in playmates in each other, many parents don't bother recruiting outside children. And even when the kid next door does come over to play, he interacts with both twins, not just one. In other words, by nature of their relationship many young twins rarely have social interactions without their cotwins. As a result, many young multiples count each other as one of their few friends. Furthermore, since MZ twins are genetically identical, they have similar interests and play patterns (they know the "rules" to all the games they concoct), and they spend more time playing with each other than DZ twins or single-born children.

Several studies have shown this. The Southern Illinois Twins and Siblings Study (SITSS) used the Child Behavior Checklist (CBCL) and observed how five-year-old twins reacted when playing with an unfamiliar peer. Each twin was matched with a same-age, same-sex singleton in a playroom laboratory and rated for inhibitions—reluctance to touch a toy first and hesitation to interact with the unknown child. The results showed that twins were significantly more unwilling to play with the toy first or even to interact with the other child than were single-born children, with identical twins behaving more shyly than their nonidentical counterparts. It's interesting to note that when asked about their twins' interactions with unfamiliar playmates prior to the experiment, parents had a totally opposite take on their kids—they saw their multiples as very sociable. Researchers concluded that since parents see their twins playing together every day, interacting prosocially with each other, they're more likely to focus on their children's positive social behaviors and less on their twins' inhibitions.

With this study's added insight, it's important for parents to step back and examine the sociability of their multiples a little more objectively and ultimately help their children develop stronger personal social skills if they are lacking. If not, problems in behavior and even language may begin to appear once the children leave the comfort of their homes and venture into a wider social world such as preschool.

Remember to never underestimate the power of friends; studies have shown that a good buddy can benefit a child's future emotional health and even help a child achieve academically as he makes his way through school. Furthermore, children who have a difficult time forming friendships may experience long-term adjustment problems later in life. Although no one knows for certain if these find-

---

From One Parent to Another

"Nathaniel and Preston (MZm) did have a shared best friend when they were young, and they have a best friend now that they share. I wouldn't say that they really have friends outside of the twinship, it's that they have the same group of friends they may just play with separately. It hasn't really affected the twinship, but I do notice that they fill each other in on what the other did with the mutual friend. It's like they don't want the other twin to miss out on what happened while they were separated."

ings translate to the multiple population, the message is clear—parents with young multiples should try to help their children form individual friendships outside the twinship.

Twins Share Friends

Is making friends a different process for multiples than it is for singletons? Absolutely. When multiples reach preschool and begin to find companions outside of the family unit, they often share their playmates with each other. This pattern often continues for many years. (Many of my survey respondents verified this.)

Furthermore, the number of friends multiples have in common varies greatly according to the twins' zygosity. In fact, a recent study of eight-year-old twins showed that identical twins have approximately 50 percent of their friends in common; nonidentical, same-sex twins share about 25 percent; while opposite-sex pairs overlap only 5 percent of their friendships. While this study answers some questions, it leaves many unanswered: Why do twins share friends? Is it because many twins—MZ in particular—have very similar likes and dislikes and therefore are drawn to the same type of people? Or is it that since most young twins hang out together and meet the same potential friends simultaneously, their social pool is more limited than if they were two single-born kids? Furthermore, is sharing friends a bad thing? Will it affect a twin's emotional and social development? No one knows for sure what the long-term implications of this study are, but a few interesting observations emerged nonetheless.

First, MZ twins overall had the most positive spin on friend sharing, taking great pleasure in it. They saw it as an important part of their twinship—even fun—with no conflict involved. Although nearly half of DZ twins found sharing friends pleasur-

able, there were certain conditions attached, such as each twin
playing with a common friend
but on different days. Therefore,
DZ twins as a group faced the
most conflicts within their twinship when building new friendships. Opposite-sex twins, who
as a group shared the fewest
friends in common, also experienced the least conflict. The
reason is that the friends they
did share were in a wider social
context (friends from a church
group, for instance) rather than a "best friend," thus eliminating any kind of rivalry.

> **From One Parent to Another**
>
> "When they were younger, Michael
> and Jennifer (DZOS) always had
> the same friends and always did
> the same things together. Now that
> they are older they each have their
> own special friends, but they still
> do things together all of the time.
> They always say that they are each
> other's best friend, and they always
> make time for each other."

Most parents I surveyed for this book had multiples that fell
within the "twin parameters" when it came to developing
friendships. That is, identical twins shared the most friends
between them with little or no conflict associated with the
arrangement (many high school identical twins still share the
majority of their friends); same-sex twins tended to diversify in
late elementary school, making separate friends and sharing
very few. My sampling showed that opposite-sex pairs seemed
to share many more friends than research indicated they would,
but several of them live in rural areas where the parents told me
that same-age, same-sex peers are harder to come by.

The Shared Best Friend

Often, too, young multiples have a common best friend. Sharing one best friend can work out (my twins have successfully
shared a best friend for three years—other survey respondents

From One Parent to Another

"Karsten and Annika (DZOS) have several of the same close friends in our neighborhood. A couple of these friends, though, try to come between my kids sometimes when they are all playing. The friend will do or say things to purposefully make either Karsten or Annika choose something different. The end result is that the friend always has one of them on his or her side."

said their children shared a best friend through middle school), but it does have a few pitfalls. Sometimes, for instance, the two-on-one triad may not work, as the single-born child may feel overwhelmed in understanding the twin dynamic and how the twins work as a couple. Furthermore, the single-born child may never really get to know each twin separately if he plays with them as a pair rather than with each one individually. Worse still is when a single-born child, not comfortable with the strength of the twin bond, deliberately tries to pit one twin against the other. Having a fourth, single-born child enter the mix can even things out. If the bunch does break off for parallel play, for instance, it will naturally dissect into two groups of two.

The other end of the spectrum is when parents of single-born children simply avoid making social contact with parents with twins altogether. They may be reluctant to have two over at once and would prefer to have just one. Yet they don't want to ask for fear of hurting feelings or insulting the twins' parent or the uninvited twin. It happens more times than you think, especially if your children are in the same classroom and a classmate prefers one twin to the other. It's an awkward position for the classmate—he wants to invite just one twin but knows he'll end up hurting the other (especially if the twin bond is tight), so in the end he chooses not to invite the twin he likes at all. Remember, attitudes are difficult to change, and if you establish your twins as an all-or-nothing proposition to families with singletons, it's very difficult to change opinions.

What Parents Can Do

Who knew that helping your twins make friends was so complicated? Actually it doesn't have to be if you take an open-for-anything approach. The key here is to help your multiples find a balance between their individuality and their intratwin relationship. All multiples do, however, need to interact with dissimilar peers, children other than their own cotwin, to help them overcome social inhibitions. In the end, it's the multiples who share some of their friends in common but develop a few separate friendships as well that seem to do the best. Here are a few ideas to help you open up a world of friendships for your multiples.

From One Parent to Another

"In tumbling class, Guinevere and Meredith (MZf) would choose one girl each week and pretty much smother her with their undivided attention even to the point that the third girl couldn't follow the teacher's instructions because my girls were so distracting. They didn't recognize that other people needed space around them. The other girls complained, and we had to teach my daughters to respect other people's space and physically separate them in the class. When they started kindergarten, they were in separate classes and each found one girl to attach themselves to. It looked to me that they were trying to replicate their twin bond when they were without their cotwin. Meredith and Guinevere would share these friends, but retained primary 'ownership.'"

- One of the best ways for you to introduce your twins to new friends is to take matters into your own hands and arrange a weekly multiple playdate. This is not for the faint of heart, mind you, especially if you have triplets and/or young boys, but the social payoff is worth it for your kids. The rules for success are simple: Set a specific time frame (no more than two hours) so there's no confusion about pick-up time, have several planned activities (set up an arts-and-crafts table, for instance) as well as free-play ideas to keep the action going, and put away any special toys that your twins may have to prevent any fighting or accidental destruction. You can even encourage more one-on-one play by having each twin buddy up with a guest to play a game together.

- Be direct and honest with parents of single-born children and reassure them that it's OK to invite your multiples over individually if they choose.

- If only one twin gets invited over for a playdate, try to arrange a separate playdate for his cotwin either at your home or someone else's.

- With proper supervision, expose your twins to kids of all ages from neighbors (invite the kids next door over for a game of basketball in the driveway) and cousins (arrange for weekend sleepovers) to children of family friends (maybe your friend has same-age children at home) and local kids at the park and public pool. The objective here is for your twins to feel comfortable with more than just their cotwin.

When One Has Trouble Making Friends

While recruiting parents of multiples for this book, I received an e-mail from a very distraught parent. "I'm the father of eight-year-old twin girls," he wrote. "We're struggling with one of my daughters. While one is well liked and popular, the other (as sweet as she is) is just not accepted in the same way." He's not alone. Other parents confided in me that one of their twins was very outgoing, amassing many friends, while the other was not as adept in social situations. For instance, one mom of nine-year-old fraternal girls spoke of her daughters drifting apart socially—one is popular in school and is invited to many sleepovers and playdates while the other girl is struggling socially having difficulty relating to her same-age peers.

It's distressing as a parent to watch a less-social child suffer emotionally in the shadow of a cotwin. The implications can be twofold: the introverted child can begin to feel inferior to her outgoing sibling and lose self-esteem while the more outgoing twin may either distance herself from her less-sociable cotwin or limit her friendships in an attempt to become her twin's protector.

There are many reasons that one multiple might be less social than the other. Some children just take longer in making long-term friendships, preferring to observe rather than participate. Still other children aren't necessarily shy but instead bossy, turning off prospective peers. When a parent discreetly steps in, though, she can help her less-sociable child build confidence and friendships. Here's how.

- Don't try to change the personality of the shy child or encourage her to be more like her sociable sister. That will only fuel resentment and sibling rivalry. Rather help her find social situations where she feels more comfortable. In other words, don't arrange playdates with the popular crowd, but rather pay attention to her cues and invite over a playmate that your child chooses.
- Before new playdates, preplan activities in which your child shines, helping to promote a more positive experience. Don't hide when the new guest arrives, hoping for the best. Remain within earshot so that you can offer guidance or a quick change of venue if a particular activity is not working out. If all goes well, try to arrange regular playdates with the same child.

- Enroll your shy child in confidence-building sports such as the martial arts or activities where she shows talent.
- Don't hold back the sociable child for the sake of the less-sociable child's feelings. Assure her that making outside friendships is a positive experience.

Can I Go Too? When One Twin Is Invited While the Other Is Not

It's coming. It may not be this year or even next year. But make no mistake, it's coming. No, I'm not talking about the next Ice Age, but the lone birthday party invitation where one of your multiples is invited and the other is not. While on a conscious level many parents understand that their school-age twins need not do everything together 24-7, subconsciously many moms feel hurt and even angry when one is excluded. Although most twins by age ten can deal with their negative feelings quite maturely, young twins need some help.

- Remember that all young children observe and learn from their parents' reactions and often assume the same attitudes later in life. Therefore, from an early age have open and ongoing dialogues with your children about the importance of and differences between both separate and shared experiences. A relaxed attitude will ultimately translate well to your multiples.
- Resist the temptation to call the host or hostess and ask if both children can attend. It's not only impolite, but it also wrongly reinforces unit thinking—that these two are an inseparable pair—to everyone involved, from your multiples to their peers. Plus, once the word is out that you'd prefer to keep them together, families with singletons will have a much harder time letting go of that idea in the future when you're ready to allow them to go out separately. (For the record:

Can I Go Too? When One Twin Is Invited While the Other Is Not *(continued)*

several parents I interviewed for this book disagreed with this approach, thinking it was cruel to invite just one twin to attend a party, especially when the children are young or if the host knows that they're twins.)

- Realize that every child will react to the situation differently. The uninvited twin may feel rejected or jealous. The invited one may feel guilty or even fearful of separating for the day. Parents should be sensitive to both sides and offer support.

- Remind the uninvited child that this is an opportunity for some special one-on-one time with Mom or Dad. Choose something meaningful to do together. (Avoid a big production though, such as going to the latest blockbuster movie that the invited twin had his heart set on seeing, too, lest he'll then feel he's being punished for going to the party.)

From One Parent to Another

"They (DZSSm) have always seemed to share friends. One weekend, a friend of Shane's invited both of them to spend the night, but Shane said that only he was going to spend the night. Kevin was a bit hurt, but I told him that sometimes Shane needs to be on his own. Kevin told me that night that it was hard to fall asleep because he's used to talking to Shane a bit every night and talking about the events that have happened throughout the day. I think they reconnect a bit each day in bed."

My Cotwin, My Friend

We've discussed at length how twins make friends outside the twinship, but what about the friendship within the twinship? How do most twins view their cotwin? Best friend or just a same-age sibling? Just how compatible are twins anyway?

Few studies have looked at how twins perceive their own friendship, but one recent study asked thirty twin pairs five to ten years in age to describe their relationships and how they viewed their cotwins. It should come as no surprise that researchers found MZ twins are the most compatible (higher cooperation with a larger number of shared activities) of all twin subgroups, followed by same-sex DZ and opposite-sex twins. The study also concluded that same-sex DZ twins experienced the most conflict (teasing, fighting, bickering) of all the subgroups. Yet fraternal female twins proved to be most interesting to researchers, describing themselves as being the most different from each other not only in their thoughts and choice of activities, but also in their dress and hairstyles. It's important to note that like many twins, the girls also enjoyed doing passive activities together such as homework and listening to music. These qualifications were merely the girls' observations of their differences rather than a statement of dislike for their cotwin, and it was these differences that helped them to define their relationship. The study didn't, however, offer an explanation for this distinction.

From the surveys that I collected for this book I, too, found that as a twin subgroup, nonidentical, same-sex girls were the most independent of each other. They seemed to rely on each other the least for companionship and looked to outside friendships more. That's not to say that these girls weren't friends—they were. Many parents reported that their DZ girls were cooperative with each other at home but had vastly different interests when it came to school and extracurricular activities. And most important, each girl was always emotionally available to her sister. Parents can use this knowledge if there's a "cooling" of their DZ daughters' relationship and realize that this is a normal stage in their twinship.

Conversely, another study found that preteen identical girls often called each other their best friend, much more often than fraternal girls. So clearly, zygosity has a lot to do with the intratwin relationship.

> **From One Parent to Another**
>
> "When they were younger, Suzanne and Elise (MZf) shared almost all the same friends. Over the past two years they've done a lot of separating, and now, while they like each other's friends, they each hang out with a different group at school. I think having outside friends has made them learn to adjust to someone who doesn't know everything about them. It also has made them appreciate each other more."

WHEN ONE TWIN DOMINATES THE OTHER

Throughout their lives many twins unconsciously take turns being in the dominant role while the other assumes a more passive position. This comes as no surprise since developmentally they probably took turns too. Although twin A walked first, twin B probably uttered "mama" first. One would master a two-wheeler, while the other became the first to spin around the driveway on in-line skates without skinning his knee. It's just the yin and yang of being a twin. Dominance and submissiveness won't have any adverse affects between the pair as long as it continues to ebb and flow throughout the years as it does in most relationships. Sometimes, however, if twins continue in their roles for prolonged periods, it can cause problems.

In the past it was believed that birth weight or birth order had a strong impact on who would dominate the twin relation-

From One Parent to Another

"I often tell people that Carissa (DZOSf) is the mom, I'm just the adult. If she could drive, she'd have no use for me at all. She's so in charge of her brother, and he allows it. The funniest thing is having them in separate classes at school with this aspect of their relationship. Kyle (DZOSm) likes having his sister mother him. In her absence, he tends to search out the little girls as friends in school who will also hand him his lunch box, sharpen his pencil, and turn in his homework. The one downside to this aspect of their relationship is when Carissa won't let Kyle answer for himself whenever he is directly asked a question. We are working on this with them because I want to foster independence with both of them and allow him to understand that he has a voice as well. I think this is about our biggest issue with the two of them."

ship—the one tipping the scales more or arriving on the scene first would win the dominant position. But one study found that it wasn't birth weight or even birth order that determined who would act as a spokesperson for the pair, but rather the sex of the child. While boys, overall, dominate physically, it's girls who usually take over the reins of the partnership in an opposite-sex twin combination.

Since little girls tend to mature faster socially and are more verbal than little boys, the position seems like a natural for a girl. And isn't it darling to see a little girl tending to her brother? Yet if the two continue in these roles of dominant female and passive male throughout their childhood and into adolescence, it can distort the female's view of manhood. If she continues to help him get dressed, help him make his bed each morning, or even count out his milk-money change as she grows up, she may come to feel that all men are helpless and inept.

DZ same-sex twins, on the other hand, may each attempt to be the dominant twin and refuse to be the passive one. On a good day, these two become friendly rivals, always striving to do better or at least keep up with the other. Unfortunately, sometimes the two can go a bit too far, constantly competing with each other about nearly everything from who got the better grade on the spelling test to who is more popular in school. It can be disrupting to a family's once peaceful symmetry as well as to intratwin harmony.

> **From One Parent to Another**
>
> "Francesca (DZOSf) has always looked after her brother and still tries to mother him at times. When they were in their early years of school, she was the one who knew what assignments were due, waited for him after class, told him when to brush his teeth or put his shoes on. He either ignored her or told her to leave him alone! We have tried to encourage his independence as they have gotten older and to do things for himself."

One interesting long-term study examined dominance and submissiveness between twins and its effect on each individual's mental health. In the study, 419 twins were evaluated several times, beginning when their mothers were pregnant through early adulthood, for changes in three separate characteristics—physical dominance, psychological dominance (decision making), and verbal dominance (acting as the pair's spokesperson). There's little surprise that more males dominated their female cotwins physically during and immediately following the school years. Girls, on the other hand, dominated their male cotwins in both the psychological and verbal domains before and during the school years. Furthermore, upon closer analysis researchers discovered that there was a connection between dominance-submissiveness and the twins' mental health. For instance, during young adulthood, psychologically submissive males in opposite-sex pairs and females from same-

---

From One Parent to Another

"One of my twins (DZSSm) is more of a natural leader. He initiates games, makes the rules, gives orders, etc. The other twin is happy to play along until he feels the dominant twin is making it unfair. Then he quits. When I've tried to make it fair or intervene in the game, it has not helped. What has helped is taking each twin aside after a confrontation and explaining to him how the behavior impacted the other and led to a falling out where no one was happy. To the dominant twin, I tell him that not allowing others to participate in the rule making or a chance to win makes others not want to play with him. To the less-dominant twin, I explain that he has a choice to not play if he doesn't feel it's fair. He can ask nicely to participate equally, and if the other doesn't allow him, he has a choice (and obligation to himself) not to play. The dominant one wants to play so will make it fair if he thinks the alternative is losing his playmate. This has helped somewhat, but it requires regular reminding."

---

sex pairs suffered from higher levels of depression, sadness, and low self-esteem. Verbally submissive males in same-sex pairs and psychologically submissive females of same-sex pairs both reported the most depressive symptoms. On the other hand, the cotwins who assumed the dominant psychological role reported high levels of nervousness. An unbalanced relationship should be taken seriously and parents should make every effort to help equalize the situation.

The study also revealed that when a twin dominated in one area, it was usually balanced by submissiveness in another area. The good news from this study was the fluidity of the intratwin relationship—the playing field leveled out with time. By the end of the school years, dominance-submissiveness decreased, with 81 percent reporting their relationship was equal in both actions and behavior.

What Parents Can Do

Parents need to step in before the dominant twin views the passive twin as a burden or the passive twin becomes so dependent on the other that she has little confidence on her own, disrupting her adolescent emotional growth and quest for autonomy. Try the following techniques to help stabilize the relationship.

- If you have a passive or dependent twin, encourage him to find a nurturing relationship outside of the twinship—a younger neighbor, for instance, or a new kid in school who could use the gentle guidance of a friend. The passive twin will gain confidence and self-esteem when someone else has the chance to look up to him much in the same way that the passive twin looks up to his cotwin.
- Allow the passive twin to play with younger children. It offers a welcome break from trying to keep up with his dominant twin.
- Teach all children to take responsibility for themselves. Discourage the dominant twin from constantly rescuing the passive twin. If they're in the same class together, never put one twin in charge of the school milk money, book orders, letter to the teacher, and so on—always give each child responsibility over his or her own. Or at the very least, allow them to take turns.
- Work on confidence building. Enroll the passive child in an activity or sport that builds self-esteem such as the martial arts.
- Be careful not to overbaby a cotwin who has a physical or cognitive disability, setting up uneven or unfair roles between twin siblings. Rather give responsibility freely to each child and see if he or she can rise to the challenge.

PROVIDING PRIVACY

Twins may not lack for attention, but they certainly lack for privacy, both psychological and physical. In my house, for instance, it's a constant battle to keep the nose of one twin out of the business of the other! "Mom? What did you just tell him?" or "What did he get on his report card?" They can't help themselves. They somehow feel that their twinship gives them the inalienable right to butt in every chance they get. Tattling figures into this as well—it seems that young twins love exposing the wrongdoings of their cotwin. Ironically, the one who's getting exposed doesn't like it until it's his turn to rat out his brother. They just don't get that it's a two-way street. It's therefore my responsibility to constantly reinforce the privacy clause in our house. For example, we stress that any misdemeanor that happens at school stays at school. I figure that if something bad enough happens, the teacher, not a cotwin, should notify me. I don't need an undercover twin working for me. And if one does break this rule, it's the tattler that gets in trouble, not the alleged bad boy.

Many twins lack physical privacy as well. From the moment of conception, multiples are always in close proximity. Most young twins share a bedroom, and it's only when adolescence approaches that many begin to ask for their own space. Parents of opposite-sex twins naturally try very hard to make this a reality, but those with same-sex twins often don't give it a second thought. And while same-sex twins may in fact get along very well with one another, providing some kind of separate space, a place they can call their own, is still important. One mom told me that although her twin daughters share a bedroom, one took over a home office, staking it out as her area to do her homework assignments and as a spot for some quiet contemplation away from the family. Another parent told me that while she felt that her daughters didn't have as much privacy as single-born children, it was one of the joys of having a twin—always having someone there to talk to.

Why Is Privacy Important?

Experts say that having time to oneself is developmentally important as it helps kids discover their own strengths and an awareness of themselves. It builds their self-confidence. It's during alone time that children learn the art of concentration, too. Studies have shown that twins are more easily distracted, having a harder time concentrating on tasks—a definite disadvantage in the classroom. They attribute this phenomenon to the fact that as soon as one twin is busy at work, her cotwin is sure to interrupt, wanting to participate too or at the very least ask questions. Furthermore, time apart can give each twin the opportunity to reflect positively on the intratwin relationship, appreciating the bond all the more.

The Parent Trap

It's tempting for twins to tattle to their parents about their cotwin's actions away from home, especially if Mom or Dad inadvertently encourages it. Although it may be done with the best intentions, sometimes parents use one multiple to clue them in on the other multiple's feelings and/or actions. Many parents do it—it's just too convenient to use one as a second pair of eyes, a nonthreatening informant. And it all starts out so innocently: "Is John in trouble with the teacher?" Or "Susan seems a bit moody lately. Do you know what's going on?" In fact, many parents confessed that one twin revealed confidences of the other twin to them. It's not done with malicious intent, just merely as a very convenient way for parents to find out what's really going on. One mom told me she has an understanding with both of her teenage girls that if there's something important that mom needs to know, she expects the other to tell.

Yet experts say you should fight the urge to engage in this covert practice. First of all, it puts a burden on the confidant since she now shares a secret about her cotwin of which the cotwin knows nothing. Besides, it's just a matter of time before the twin in question will figure out that something is going on behind her back, perhaps causing a breach of trust between the pair. A better alternative is to work toward a loving and trusting relationship with all your children, and if something concerns you about one of them, simply ask her in private.

Conversely, some multiples feel the need to offload personal feeling about their cotwin: "He's so immature. You should see him act out in class." Or "She's so dorky! I'm embarrassed to be seen with her!" This, too, can be tricky ground, but as long as you remain impartial, acting as a patient listener rather than stepping in to try to fix the situation, no harm can come of it.

What Parents Can Do

With another same-age sibling always present, it's sometimes hard to give your twins a sense of privacy, but it is possible.

Here are a few ideas to get you started.

- Deal with tattling quickly and privately. The sooner you establish and maintain a "no tattling" rule, the sooner your multiples will give it up. Set up household rules pertaining to privacy issues. For instance, who's allowed to view your children's tests or report cards? What's your closed-door or bathroom policy?
- If you can't offer each twin his or her own bedroom, try changing roommates every six months or every year, pairing one twin with another single-born family member. At the very least, foster a bedroom environment where each twin has his or her own special area and belongings.
- Make weekly private chats part of the family routine and keep the conversation between you and the twin who's in your company. One mom of opposite-sex, teenage twins instated weekly "private time." After school, one child would go to his or her room while the other stayed in the kitchen to chat. This mom would ensure privacy by closing the hallway door and placing a portable radio up against the door. (She said her daughter loved to eavesdrop.)
- Cultivate your teenage twins' thirst for a bit more privacy by encouraging them to find a weekend part-time job or attend separate summer camps. A plead for privacy may just be their way of asking for more independence.

From Wombmates to Roommates: Secrets to Successfully Sharing a Bedroom

Even if it's impossible for you to offer each twin his or her own bedroom, there are clever ways to give the illusion of privacy when two share the

(continued on next page)

same space. It just takes a bit of imagination and a little bit of sweat. So roll up your sleeves and get to work!

- Plan it right. Pick up a few design magazines or books to get ideas.
- Get your multiples' input (within reason, of course) on what they'd like to see. Find out what's important to them, such as having separate shelf space or a quiet reading corner, and try to accommodate each child's individual wishes.
- Even in a small bedroom, try to visually divide the space using a bookcase, curtain, or even a freestanding partition, providing each child with a private space and the appearance of his or her own room, no matter how small.
- Don't forget separate storage containers, the more the better. For instance, instead of one dresser, try captain's beds where clothes drawers are under each mattress. A filing cabinet with separate drawers is a good idea, too. It gives each child a place to stash secret documents, and it also teaches them how to organize their busy lives!
- Encourage your twins to discuss and draft a list of roommate rules and post it for both to see. For instance, they should talk over such things as quiet time for studying, who will be responsible for dusting and vacuuming, and visiting guests. (If one invites a friend for a sleepover, for instance, will his cotwin be invited, too?) When things are clearly spelled out, it prevents arguments and bad feelings down the road.
- If you have triplets and only two bedrooms, you may want to consider turning one room into a dorm where all three can sleep and use the other room for studying and socializing where each child gets her own desk and seating area. Or try the switch-off approach—

From Wombmates to Roommates:
Secrets to Successfully Sharing a Bedroom (continued)

every six months one girl moves into her own room and the other two share the second. One mom of triplet girls and another younger, single-born daughter and only two bedrooms has everyone change rooms every year so that eventually all girls will be roommates at some point.

SOMETIMES "I" AND SOMETIMES "WE"

The road to individuality and separate autonomy can be rough at times and may seem contradictory, too. It can be a bit tricky to promote independence while encouraging sibling love. You can help pave the path for your multiples by challenging them to discover what's special within themselves. By celebrating both their differences and their similarities, your children will not only build a healthy view of themselves but will also appreciate their bond all the more.

3

Double Discipline

If you're like me, you've probably heard the comment, "Twins? Now that's double trouble!" one too many times. Or perhaps you're fed up when you turn on the television only to see some silly sitcom depicting the parents of multiples on the brink of a nervous breakdown as their out-of-control group proceeds to tear through the house. So why is it that when it comes to behavior, multiples always get such a bad rap? Why are they always stereotyped as mischievous, bad-to-the-bone bruisers? Is there some truth to it? Are twins really double trouble?

Personally, I don't think multiples are born to be bad. Just like single-born children, twins need rules and guidelines to help them learn self-control and to know what's appropriate behavior and when. The difference between the two groups, however, is simply numbers—it's a bit easier to break the rules when you have someone else who's willing to break them with you.

MANAGING MULTIPLE CHILDREN

Bad puns and poorly written television shows aside, disciplining two or more same-age children is more challenging than directing two or more single-born children of different ages. There are a couple of very logical reasons why. First of all, with twins you have two children at exactly the same developmental stage. Young twins, for example, are still learning the art of negotiation, taking turns, and sharing. Therefore when they both see a toy they want neither one is willing to step down. On the contrary—they'll both fight to the death for that toy! Result? Screaming, crying, kicking, biting—you've seen it before; I don't need to go on. But preschool twins aren't the only discipline challenge. Just wait until the teenage years. With adolescent twins, two times the hormones usually mean two times the drama! Translation: lots of sulky faces, door slams, and screaming matches.

When you have a group of young multiples playing together, they can also put their clever little minds together and come up with all sorts of new and exciting games, many of which are dangerous. I remember once my guys were playing in the backyard and they decided to do a treasure hunt. Great idea. Unfortunately, they dug in the recycling bin and found bits of broken glass that they proceeded to hide in the garden. (After I had recovered from the shock of discovering them digging in the dirt for jagged shards, they explained that they needed something small to hunt for and the glass seemed like a good idea.) Other stories I've heard revolve around twins giving each other a boost up to unlock front doors, get into cupboards where the good china lay hidden, and even climb out of playpens or cribs.

Then of course there's the Zen factor with twins—it's the term I use when my boys are so "in the zone" or in tune with each other that they simply can't hear me when I try to interrupt. Their voices get louder, their actions get sillier, and someone—always with the intent of entertaining the other—goes over the top and does something he shouldn't. Moving on down the list: there are other twins who misbehave due to the "celebrity factor." Constantly taking center stage in the family and drawing attention everywhere they go, these doppelgängers can suddenly transform into spoiled stage kids if they don't get their way. This tends to be a bigger problem when twins are the only children in the family. And let's not overlook the "fertility factor" either. Some parents having suffered through years of infertility now are suddenly blessed with not one but two babies. Still clinging to the prenatal fantasy of the perfect family, they simply let bad behavior slide. They have waited so long for children that now they simply have a harder time enforcing the rules for fear of rocking the boat. And finally, there's worn-out Mom and Dad. Let's face it—it just gets tiring constantly governing the kids, so sometimes we turn a deaf ear to it all. Unfortunately, when you're not consistent with discipline, your kids pick that up and use it to their advantage.

Yet it's not all bad news. The biggest bonus for parents with multiples is that twins keep each other company. When they're occupied they're less likely to whine and negatively demand attention. In fact, many twins keep each other in line by reminding each other of the rules. They police each other. In my house, I often hear one twin say to the other, "Hey, you'd better not. Mom will be mad." And sure enough, the devious action stops and play resumes in more productive ways (OK, so not always).

Toy Tantrums

From the time they can crawl all the way up through the school years, multiples will inevitably argue over toys. Twin multiples

From One Parent to Another

"When Sheila and Virginia (DZSSf) argued over toys, we'd put the item in a time out. Every toy we'd buy, every gift they'd get, we had to look at it and think—not just in terms of safety—but how are they going to fight over this? We opted out of a lot of choices because it just wasn't worth the trouble of having it in the house."

can get into it over any silly object—before you know it, fighting for the blue trike soon gives way to duking it out over a coveted Game Boy cartridge.

To counter the toy wars, parents with preschool multiples should stick with items that have many different parts such as building blocks, Legos, paint sets, and so on. More parts mean everyone has a chance to participate fully without competing for a certain toy. (In families where multiples are younger than three years, parents need to take care when choosing toys with many parts as they can be a choking hazard.) Although tempting, resist the urge to buy two of everything. Not only is it expensive and require tons of room to store, it rarely solves the problem since twins always want what a cotwin has in his possession at that moment. And what happens when one of the two identical toys breaks? You're sure to have a screaming match on your hands. Instead, many parents opt for two complementary items such as a football and a soccer ball, a dump truck and a fire truck, or two different Barbie dolls.

Fostering Cooperation in Young Multiples

Contrary to what many may think, cooperation doesn't mean a child does exactly as an adult tells him to do. Actually, it's a process where the child learns to balance his needs and desires with those of others. Cooperation, the art of give-and-take, is a skill that all young children need to master, but it takes practice. And for multiples who play together day in and day out and spend most of their young lives together, teaching cooperation between them can help reduce conflict and avoid more complex arguments further down the road (as well as a few headaches for Mom and Dad). But how do you teach it?

- Demonstrate how to take turns through games when they're very young. Sit everyone in a circle and roll either a ball or truck to one child. Once he has it in his hands, shout out, "It's Suzy's turn. Roll it to Suzy." Congratulate him as he rolls it to his cotwin. Encourage Suzy to roll it to you since it's your turn, and so on.

- Explain conflict resolution (this is most effective when you do so when both children are calm). If there's a problem or disagreement, whether over a toy or which TV show to watch, don't step in and fix it but rather ask each of your multiples to name the problem. Let each one come up with a solution that he thinks is fair to both children. This way each child is part of the solution and has a stake in its outcome. Congratulate them when they come up with a compromise that's agreeable to both. (If they can't agree, give each a cooling-off period in separate locations and then have them try again.)

- Offer choices that give each child a sense of control and power instead of strict edicts that they're sure to rebel against. Instead of saying, "It's peanut butter or nothing for lunch," try "Which way would you prefer to have your peanut butter sandwich, on wheat toast or white bread?"

- Help them to problem solve. Instead of saying, "You can't wear a summer dress today. It's too cold," try "I think you may be too cold in that dress. How can you fix that?" She may walk out with a turtleneck sweater layered underneath, but she solved the problem!

- Solo play is OK. Just because your young multiples hang out together all day doesn't mean they always want to play together; every once in a while they may prefer to play by themselves. If a child would like to go off by himself for a bit, encourage him to do so, and help his cotwin understand the need for alone time.

- Older multiples could use a refresher course on cooperation, too. Be direct in your wishes. Instead of saying, "I sure would like it if my children would clean up after themselves," try "When we get inside, please hang up your backpacks in your bedrooms." Like younger children, older kids respond well to choices, too, but you can add a few twists to them such as the time choice ("When would you like to start your homework, right after school or a half hour later?") or sequence choice ("Don't forget you need to practice piano, study for your math test, and set the table. Whichever order you choose is fine with me.")

Intratwin Bickering—Should You Step In?

Every child has his own technique for getting Mom's or Dad's attention and getting a cotwin in trouble. Twins have a great way of finding their cotwin's weaknesses and exploiting them to their advantage. In my house, one twin is a master at quietly instigating trouble. He knows that with just a minimal amount of effort and button pushing in all the right places, he can make his cotwin scream out in angry frustration, making the shouter look like the out-of-control offender. In the past, we've reprimanded the screamer thinking he was the culprit until we caught on that was exactly what the quiet instigator was hoping for. Wising up, we have since changed our strategy and butt out.

When parents constantly step in and referee twin squabbles both big and small, the children never learn how to settle their differences on their own. ("Why compromise over the TV remote when Mom will take my side?") During the first hint of a fight, they'll look to you to mediate rather than think of a way to settle it for themselves. Furthermore, when Mom or Dad gets involved in sibling conflict it usually means that now you have to decide how to settle the disagreement, and often that means siding with one child over the other—a big no-no since it can look like favoritism and only incite more rivalry between the pair. ("See? Mom agrees with me

> ### From One Parent to Another
>
> "If Kate and Victoria (MZf) fight and hurt each other, I usually have them separate and go to their rooms to cool down. I say they can come out when they each have written a short note of apology to the other, the 'shake hands and make up' approach. This seems to work, and it is amazing what they write to each other. Sometimes it takes a long time for them to reconcile; sometimes it's instant. But I always put the power into their hands."

and not you!") Instead parents should take to the sidelines and keep an ear out for name-calling (not permitted) or physical violence (never allowed). Only then should you step in with consequences or to escort each child to a separate room for a cooling-off period. It's OK to listen to each child's complaints, but don't react. It's important not to take sides but rather help each child understand and listen to the complaints of the other.

What Parents Can Do

You may get tired of enforcing the rules, but unfortunately, that's exactly what it takes. We often forget how to parent properly and find ourselves yelling at our kids as if we were five years old and in bad need of a nap. Discipline isn't all about punishing—it's really about encouraging good behavior, teaching and

---

From One Parent to Another

"I learned early on—although it took several lessons—to just walk away and let Evelyn and Alice (zygosity unknown) work it out. If I stayed or paid attention, the argument would just escalate or I'd be left standing in the middle talking to myself since now they were off giggling. If they were fighting over a toy or if something broke and I would try to mediate between the two to help them work it out, pretty soon they'd start making faces at each other and then be having a wonderful time hugging and calling each other their pet names while I'm left feeling silly for getting involved."

---

modeling what's acceptable and discouraging what's not. Flexibility is key when disciplining—not everything works for every kid. And that's an especially important point for parents of multiples—discipline each child based on her personality and what works for her. Still, there are a few basic parenting principles that we can all live by. Here's a quick rundown.

- Keep your cool as well as a good attitude. You've heard the expression, "Pick your battles." Let the annoying everyday stuff slide and save your energy for something more offensive. Discipline doesn't mean you have to win every disagreement with your children. It isn't about having power over them. Admit when you've overreacted to a situation and move on.
- Provide daily routines when it comes to homework, daily household chores, bedtime, and so forth. When everyone knows what to expect and when, it cuts down on stress as well as bickering.
- Consistency and follow-through are king. If it's not OK to play ball in the house, it's *never* OK to play ball in the

house. If you say, "If you throw that ball in the house again, you won't be able to play PlayStation for a week," you'd better back up your speech with action when he throws the ball in the house again. When you are consistent with rules and following through with consequences when the rules are broken, kids learn quickly that your word is law.

- Outline very clear, nonnegotiable, age-appropriate consequences to your children for any wrongdoing and make sure you stick to them! And no, they can't win the privilege back; remember that you need to firmly enforce the consequence you set.

- Never punish both children simply because you didn't see who did the crime. Try a little mental strong-arming instead. "I know the guilty party will step forward and take responsibility for his actions" is the mantra in my home. OK, so I say it at least ten times over the course of an hour, but it works.

- Never compare one twin's behavior to the other as a way of shaming ("Look at how nicely she's putting her toys away. Why can't you do that, too?") or as an incentive ("Whoever puts her clothes away first gets the last Popsicle"). Instead approach the task as a team effort ("Let's see if you boys can put more groceries away than me").

- Notice and praise good behavior. I know this one can be tough to see sometimes, but try to spot even a hint of positive conduct and praise it enthusiastically for all to hear. When your multiples are cooperating nicely with each other, tell them so; they'll be more likely to repeat it in the future.

- If one of your multiples suddenly starts using negative, attention-seeking behavior, perhaps it's his way of saying he needs some "Mom time." Many parents have found that simply spending more alone time with the rascal, giving him loving, positive attention, helps to curb his naughty ways.

From One Parent to Another

"The problem comes when the passive child feels a cross-eyed look is punishment enough and the more dominant child has the 'bring it on' attitude. We've had to assert discipline based upon the child and the infraction, not just the infraction alone. This has posed a problem administering different consequences for the same violation in front of two children. For example, once I found a pile of laundry that I had just folded dumped in the middle of the floor because Carissa (DZOSf) wanted a particular shirt and Kyle (DZOSm) offered to get it for her. When she entered the room in the shirt, I immediately knew where she had gotten it. I had Carissa refold the laundry and place it back in the basket, and Kyle had to sit in time-out with his dad. Carissa refused to refold because Kyle was the one who had dumped it and she began to tantrum because he didn't have to refold."

Charting a Course

Sometimes children get locked into bad behavior—they've successfully gotten a reaction, albeit negative, from Mom or Dad for so long that it's difficult to change. But we've all heard the power of positive reinforcement. If you reward the good and ignore the bad, it doesn't take long for a child to realize that the good behavior also gets parental attention, but this time with lots of love thrown in— what he or she was going after all along. And when young children are involved, nothing excites or encourages them more than colorful stickers.

If you're having a difficult time getting your young multiples to follow the rules, head to the stationery store and stock up on a variety of exciting stickers (choose ones that they can relate to—superheroes, for instance) and a large sheet of poster board.

First order of business— choose the negative behavior you'd like to stop, such as hitting. (For the best results, work on eliminating only one or two offenses at a time, otherwise it will

be too overwhelming for a child
to internalize.) Be sure to choose
a different behavior issue per
twin so as not to call too much
attention to any one child.

Next, divide your poster
board in half with each child's
name printed at the top. List the
next fourteen to twenty-one
days down the side (each day
can be divided into morning and
afternoon in the beginning since
it's easier to be good for shorter
periods of time). Hang your chart in an important location
where all family members can see it, such as in the kitchen.

From One Parent to Another
"I did time-outs early on, but I had difficulty enforcing them. We used to have a baby gate on the stairs, and I would put one of them (MZm) behind the gate as if he were in prison, but then the other one would come over and socialize! It was really hard to make it a real time-out."

Then start to notice the good behavior and praise it enthusiastically out loud for all to hear. At the end of the morning or
the day (whichever you have chosen), if your child has made a
successful effort in behaving, hand him a sticker with cheerful
fanfare. After four or five stars, award a small prize such as a
treat, a dime, new crayons, etc. Never take a star away for bad
behavior (if you just can't look the other way, calmly give the
offender a time-out in his room). If a star wasn't earned, keep
the space blank.

After three weeks you can gradually fade out the system,
replace another negative behavior, or celebrate your twins' success with a special day out.

TWEEN AND TEEN MULTIPLES:
ARE THEY HARDER TO DISCIPLINE?

Just when your young multiples have finally learned to share
their toys, treat each other with an adequate amount of respect,

Teaching Manners

Good manners aren't just for the dining room table—teaching your children to be polite, kind, gracious, and empathetic toward others will help them in the classroom and on the playground. They'll be more able to resolve conflicts in appropriate ways by themselves, and kids with good social skills will have an easier time making and keeping friends, too. So start 'em young and remember, no elbows on the table.

- Model good behavior and your children will get a front-row seat as to how it's done. Compassionate, caring parents usually raise compassionate, caring kids. If you prefer to cuss out every other car on the freeway as you tailgate for a mile just to teach them a lesson, you're more likely going to find yourself in the principal's office every week explaining your son's bad behavior in class.
- Make "please," "thank you," and "excuse me" a part of your family's everyday vocabulary, and don't be afraid to use gentle reminders. ("What do you say when someone offers you something to drink?") If they're about to attend a social function that's new to them such as a wedding, role-play the appropriate behavior (trust me, they'll think it's fun), acting out various situations they may encounter that day.
- Teach how to lose and win with dignity. Failing is a tough one since no kid likes to lose at anything, especially to a cotwin. Gently remind the loser that she should shake hands with the winner and offer congratulations even though she'd prefer to walk away. Praise her effort, even if her attempt is less than perfect. And conversely, let her know that it's OK to feel happy when she wins, but she shouldn't boast or brag.
- Remember, manners are a two-way street. Treat your children with the same respect with which you want them to treat others. You can't be rude to your kids and then count on them to go out in the world and speak kindly to others.

and sit at the dinner table with their napkins actually in their laps, *Wham!* Puberty hits. They may sit up straight at the table, but now they have scowls on their faces.

The teen years are a rocky time for many kids as each tests the waters of impending adulthood, but for multiples it's also a time of breaking away from not only parents but also one's cotwin. This can cause conflict not only between parents and child but within the twin dyad as well. It can be a difficult time for parents, too, as it's challenging trying to relate to the one who's rebelling—it's much easier to feel closer to an obedient child. It helps for parents to tap into their dwindling reserve of patience. Just like in their tempestuous toddler days, teen twins need a clear set of rules and limits. Kids, especially young teens, have an uncanny knack for picking up on when parents are uncertain or reluctant to enforce a certain rule. And if you as parents don't present a united front to your kids, they'll put the squeeze on and never give up until you acquiesce. Although it may seem counterintuitive, when your rebellious child screams "I hate you" and acts in other appalling ways, she actually needs you even more. Eventually she will come around and show love again. In fact, many twins looking back have actually shown appreciation for the fair discipline their parents enforced even though they were anything but delighted by it at the time.

> **From One Parent to Another**
>
> "One always tries to defend the other when he gets in trouble. If I have to ground one of them, it's really tough on the one who has the freedom as opposed to the one who's restricted. When Andrew (DZSSm) was grounded, Jeffrey (DZSSm) kept asking if I'd make an exception for his brother. I think he felt guilty because he knew he was going to have fun with all their friends and Andrew would have to stay home."

From One Parent to Another

"Samantha and Alex (DZSSf) have such a connection that when I discipline one, they both feel the pain. It is the strangest thing because this has been going on since they were babies. For instance, Sam came in and told me that Alex was mad and ripped up two of her posters. I was very angry and told Alex that she needed to give Sam two of her posters to cover the ones she ripped up. Sam immediately started to defend Alex and wanted to take her tattling back. She started to say that she didn't like the posters anyway and that she could live without them. I turned to Sam and said, 'Why did you tell on her if you didn't want her in trouble?' She started to cry and said she didn't want her to be in trouble. It's always been this way—when they were younger if I yelled at one, they would both go into their bedroom and cry."

Twin Type Discipline Challenges

Opposite-sex pairs and male-male-female triplets sets can experience challenges that other twin types won't. If the female multiple matures faster—and most likely she will since girls usually advance faster than boys both physically and socially—she may become a wild, boy-crazy teen while her brothers hang out at home watching Friday night TV with a bowl of popcorn. In other words, a boy at this age may toe the line while the girl revels in rebellion.

For many nonidentical, same-sex twins, adolescence brings on a strong yearning for individuality, and as the need to differentiate from one's cotwin increases, many twins find themselves moving in opposite directions. This can lead to bickering as each tries to feel better about the path he's chosen. Many same-sex, teenage twins become polar opposites during adolescence. In an attempt to be seen as different, many twins choose different subjects or sports to excel in. But if one twin feels overshadowed by a high-achieving cotwin, the former may seek negative attention by acting out in class and at home. If he thinks he can never measure up or compete at the same level, he won't try to and may simply choose to do the opposite. Sometimes he may even feel stuck in his role as the bad boy, not knowing how to change, especially if Mom or Dad continues to reinforce his role by giving his negative behavior ample attention. (Read more about the couple effect in Chapter 7, "When They Reach Puberty: Multiples as Teenagers.")

What Parents Can Do

The teenage years are a time of enormous change and growth. Although conflict between siblings and within the family is a normal part of adolescence, it's how children resolve their differences that matters. Settling arguments constructively helps to build social skills in the art of negotiation and compromise. It can be a bit tricky finding the best formula for helping your multiples gain the self-control they'll need to function as adults. Most of the same rules apply as when they were little, but here is some extra food for thought.

- Give privileges based on maturity, not age. Just because they were born on the same day doesn't mean they're ready to accept adult responsibility at the same time. Tread carefully though—never use one twin's privileges as an incentive for the other to straighten up. Not only will this be counterproductive, as the less mature child will undoubtedly try to live up to your low expectations of him, it will spark a rivalry between the pair. Instead calmly explain the discrepancy to the less mature twin in private where he'll have the chance to vent his frustration and you can offer support and ways in which he can get his behavior under control.

- Don't rush to save your teenager from the brink of disaster—allow for consequences to play out naturally. If your son consistently forgets his homework at school, instead of writing a note to the teacher or worse, letting his cotwin bail him out, let your son go to school unprepared and accept the penalty. He'll quickly learn to take responsibility for his own actions.

- Help teenage children develop and pursue more adult interests. Encourage an appreciation for music, art, or sports. Teens who are productively involved in the arts and sports have less need to act out in unhealthy ways or to spend idle time bickering with their cotwin.

- Curb the criticism and praise accomplishments. Teens who are constantly reprimanded and continually reminded to do better end up "checking out." Instead of trying to improve, they often give up since they feel they can never meet a parent's expectations. A better course of action is to commend the areas where they excel.

- Although they may seem reluctant, teens need more of a parent's time and attention now, not less. Set up a monthly parent-child "date night" and take each child out individually for a grown-up evening such as dinner and a movie. One mom said since her teenage son had a hard time with the date concept, she referred to it as their "appointment." Whatever you call it, do it regularly.

YOU'VE GOT IT UNDER CONTROL

Teaching your children how to behave responsibly is one of the most challenging (and often frustrating) realms of parenting, and when you have multiples, it requires a bit more moxie. Although "double trouble" is a Hollywood concoction, there are a few more problems that parents of toddler and teen mul-

---

From One Parent to Another

"Both sets of twins (DZSSf) got privileges when each was ready, regardless of where the other twin was developmentally. I didn't like pushing them to catch up with each other, or anyone else for that matter. They are individuals and should grow and mature at their own pace."

---

tiples face. It takes age-appropriate rules and consequences and plenty of repetition before good behavior sinks in. But most important, remember that all twins are different. Even though they were born on the same day, what works well with one may not work with the other.

4

Multiples and Education

By far, one of the most complex issues facing school-age multiples and their parents centers on education. Even before many twins are walking, their parents are pondering a host of questions, from whether they should separate their twins into different classrooms to what to do if one child is ready for kindergarten while the other isn't.

Schools are being affected by the rapid rise in twinning and higher-order multiples, too. Most school districts have found themselves without any written policy when it comes to placement of multiples and therefore arbitrarily separate them. Yet very few long-term studies have been done on the psychological effects of classroom separation for multiples, highlighting the need for more research on the subject.

In addition to the ever-debated separation issue, there are other educational concerns exclusive to multiples. For instance, overall, twins experience more reading and language problems than single-born children do. Many young twins are also more socially immature, and they often struggle with fine motor skills, due in part to their premature birth. This doesn't mean that every pair will have a tough time of it or that multiples are any less intelligent than single-born children. It just means that as a group they're more susceptible to these issues and experience more of them. The good news is that once you educate yourself on the possible problems, you're more likely to intervene before they have a chance to hinder your twins' development.

In this chapter, it's all sorted out for you with the most recent information currently available on multiples in school. Still, it's not a clear-cut issue. Even parents of multiples often disagree about what's in the best interest of twin (and even triplet) children. So how do you know you've made the right decision for your children? The key is to know your kids and observe them carefully. After all, you are the best judge of your children and how they will respond to certain situations. So do your homework and don't be afraid to ask questions.

KINDERGARTEN READINESS

Why is there so much attention on kindergarten readiness these days? For better or worse, kindergarten is a very different institution from when we were kids. The days of cutting and pasting have given way to phonics and writing. No longer a place where kids just learn to socialize well with others and to separate successfully from Mom, today's kindergarten is much more focused on cognitive learning, although socialization is still part of the package.

While signing your twins up for preschool as soon as they're able to attend is a good idea, you shouldn't be in a huge rush to enroll them in kindergarten. Your twins may meet the minimum age requirement for school (it varies from state to state),

The Role of Preschool

How many times when your multiples were very young did you opt to stay home and let your little ones play by themselves rather than trying to get everyone dressed, fed, and out the door for a playdate? With young multiples underfoot, sometimes it's just too strenuous and too exhausting to get out on a regular basis. It's not unusual for parents of multiples to take a complacent role when it comes to early socialization. And while it's great that each child has a built-in playmate or two, some multiples lag behind singletons developmentally because of it.

That's where preschool comes in. Not only does preschool allow each twin to develop socially, but the informal setting also encourages receptive and expressive language development. Here's how to make it a positive experience for each child.

- Meet with the preschool teacher prior to the first day to talk about your multiples' special educational needs and areas of concern such as language acquisition and fine motor skills.
- Make it easy for classmates to identify each child individually by dressing your twins differently. If they're identical (MZ) twins, try color-coding their outfits—red and blues for one child, greens and yellow for the other, for instance.
- Consider having them attend different days or allowing each to go one day a week alone while keeping her cotwin at home. This gives the child at school an opportunity to develop her own social skills and build her language proficiency while the child at home gets Mom or Dad all to herself (something that most twins greatly need and sadly lack).
- Remember that preschool is only for a short amount of time each week and that most development happens at home. Make home a fun, rich environment filled with lots of books, music, and art.

but you may want to hold off for another year if your twins are still struggling verbally or socially, especially if they're on the tail end of the cutoff date (summer and fall babies). Remember, too, if your twins were born prematurely, they actually lag chronologically behind their single-born peers by one, two, or even three months, giving you even more reason to avoid a hasty enrollment.

How Can You Tell if They're Ready?

One of the most important clues to tell if your multiples are ready for the rigors of kindergarten is their language development. Make sure their speech is on target. Do they talk your ear off? Love to tell you stories? Sing and recite nursery rhymes? If not, you may want to take a step back and reconsider an early kindergarten enrollment. Research shows that when twins lag behind linguistically, they're usually less sociable with other children, too. If you're unsure of your multiples' speech development, have them evaluated by a speech therapist or pathologist. (Check with your school district to see if the district offers this service.)

Even if your multiples are great little orators, look for other signs of readiness, such as adequate fine and gross motor skills (throw a ball, hold a pencil correctly, and at least attempt to write letters), academic sense (count to ten, identify colors and simple shapes, repeat a story using details), and personal and social skills (get along with others, wash their hands, listen and follow rules). And finally, listen to your gut. Sure, they may be intelligent little kids, but look at the whole picture and ask yourself, "Are they developmentally ready for kindergarten?"

No one can really help a child get ready for kindergarten, but as a parent there are a few simple things that you can do to gently steer them in the right direction. For instance, encourage your young twins to work independently on tasks and not rush to be the first one done. This will not only help them learn the art of concentration, but it will also aid them when it comes time to learn to read. Inspire them to be curious students by asking them questions about the world around them. ("Why do you think the windows are frosty this morning?") Clue them in on what you're doing every day from grocery shopping ("How many apples should we buy today?") to writing on the family calendar ("How many more days is it until your birthday?"). And it is very important to make reading aloud a priority every day.

When One Twin Is Ready for Kindergarten While the Other Is Not

It's not uncommon for one twin to be ready for kindergarten while her cotwin isn't. Yet before you jump to any conclusions, make sure you're not comparing one twin's readiness to the other. While one twin may appear to be less able than her cotwin, the slower twin may be within the normal range. The more important question to ask is, how does she measure up against her peers? Does she lag behind the other children in preschool, or is she right on target with the group?

Realize, too, that if you decide to keep only one twin home an extra year while sending her cotwin off to kindergarten, it sets into motion a lifelong difference between the pair. It may not matter so much in the younger grades but will have a huge impact on their relationship once they reach adolescence. Furthermore, it's not uncommon for the developmentally slower twin to catch up and eventually pass the twin who was once thought of as advanced.

One solution is to keep both home for an extra year, especially if they're summer or fall babies. In addition, have the struggling twin evaluated by a professional to see exactly what you're up against. She may simply be a "late bloomer" who needs just a bit more attention and help to get on target.

Speech: How Language Acquisition Affects Learning

Most children start talking between the ages of eighteen months and three years. Yet did you know that twins begin to exchange signs—the basis for language—with each other well before this time frame? Twins have an enormous capacity for preverbal and nonverbal communication, but if parents don't actively participate verbally with their multiples—leaving them instead to copy each other's linguistic mistakes—the result can be autonomous language, or idioglossia. Although nearly 40 percent of twins—and a higher percentage of triplets—develop some form of autonomous language, in most cases it disappears quickly.

Overall, preschool twins experience delayed speech more often than singleton children of the same age. And boys, who on average lag behind girls in language development, are even more at risk. At thirty months of age, for instance, some male multiples are approximately a whopping eight months behind singletons in expressive language. They have trouble articulating their words, often leaving off the first or last consonant, they tend to form less complex sentences with fewer words, and they usually speak louder, too (perhaps since they're so used to competing to get the attention of an adult).

Fortunately language problems manifest themselves when twins are young but usually diminish as they mature. The bad news, however, is the residual effects speech delay has on later speech-related tasks such as reading, writing, and even spelling. Research strongly suggests that there is a connection between speech acquisition and learning.

So why are multiples more susceptible to speech problems? It's not that twins are any less able to speak. In fact, in studies where twins were adopted into separate families, their verbal IQs were on target with single-born children. There are many theories as to why they have more speech problems than singletons, but researchers agree on several contributing factors. For instance, since twins intrinsically understand each other's gestures and habits, they may have less incentive to learn to speak. Parents of young children are a busy lot, too, and tend to answer their twins' questions briefly, using directives rather than engaging in a conversation. In other words, they may not give their twins enough "air time." The twins themselves sense that they have just a limited amount of time to get their point across and may compete with each other to be heard by Mom or Dad by speaking quickly and in the process omitting some consonants. And since young twins are also the perfect playmates, twins just don't get the same exposure to a wide range of adults and other children as singletons do, thereby limiting their need for verbal communication. And finally, twins serve as poor speech models to each other, often imitating each other's verbal faux pas. It's the combination of all these factors that sometimes causes a delay in speech for multiples.

Let's keep this all in perspective, however. It's important to note that not all twins will suffer from delayed speech. In fact, some twins who have ample opportunity to communicate with adults and have a large peer base are superior in language development to their singleton counterparts. And even if your twins do experience some form of delay, it doesn't necessarily mean that they'll struggle to read. With that said, here are a few tips to ensure that your twins have the gift of gab.

- Get that conversation going. Talk it up, ad nauseam, but avoid speaking to your children as a pair and instead talk to them individually, resisting the urge to speak mostly with the one whose language is more advanced.

- Give each child who is speaking your full attention and eye contact. If one asks for something, such as a glass of milk, don't automatically get a drink for both. Allow the other twin a chance to ask as well.
- Never allow the "talkative" twin to interrupt or speak for the "quieter" twin.
- Gently correct syntax errors by repeating your child's sentence using the proper speech. For instance, if one of your multiples says, "I outside go and play backyard," answer with, "Oh, you said you'd like to go outside and play in the backyard?"
- Expand your twins' circle of friends by introducing them to a variety of children. This is where preschool comes in pretty handy. (As mentioned previously, you might consider having them attend on alternating days so they can each reach out verbally to fellow classmates.)
- While autonomous language may be fascinating, it should not be encouraged. (After all, if a single-born child used autonomous language, most parents would seek intervention immediately.)
- Match words with the visual cues. For instance, don't just say "bird," but point to one at the same time.
- Sing and read stories and rhyming poems. (Busy moms can take advantage of books on tape during car rides, encouraging their children to follow along with the printed page.)
- Pay attention to possible problems and get a professional diagnosis as soon as you suspect speech difficulties.

SEPARATE OR TOGETHER?

The $64,000 question on every parent's mind with young multiples is whether to separate them or keep them together once they hit kindergarten. In fact, it's the number one cause of conflict between parents of multiples and school administrators.

Before we dive into the subject further, however, let's once again consider the life of a typical set of young twins. Most do just about everything together. Many share the same bedroom as well as bedtime. They eat meals, bathe, and play together. So when it comes time for school—a huge adjustment for any child—twins must not only learn to separate from their parents for the first time, but they also must separate from their cotwin. The transition will be harder for some than for others. For multiples who have been encouraged from an early age to make their own friends, have spent ample time apart, or simply enjoy doing activities away from each other, separation may not be a big issue. For other twins, identical twins (MZ) especially, who may have had little experience with separation or whose bond is inherently stronger than most, being in different classrooms may be traumatic.

Asking your young twins whether they'd like to be separated or stay together can be tricky because they don't have much school experience from which to draw a conclusion. Some twins may feel reluctant to express their true feelings, asking to be together simply because it's what they know or because they fear hurting the feelings of their sibling. Parents can get feedback by asking each his opinion separately, but they should also carefully observe their children in different social situations to assess each individual's needs before ultimately making the final decision. It's interesting to note, too, that whenever there's a problem with multiples—speech and reading, rivalry, social immaturity—schools always recommend to separate the two. Yet does separation cure every ill? Absolutely not. Before hastily separating your twins in the hope that all difficulties will work out, combat the disability or problem first. That's not to say that separation won't help—often it will. Just make it part of the solution, not the sole solution.

"One-size-fits-all" may work when it comes to rain ponchos, but not when it comes to multiples and learning. Just as every single-born child has unique educational needs, so does each twin, triplet, and quadruplet. Unfortunately most school districts continue with a one-size-fits-all policy in regard to multiples and classroom placement. And that usually entails separating them. While separation may have worked exceptionally well for one set of twins, it may be disastrous for the next. The most successful school districts have adopted a flexible policy, one where each set of multiples is evaluated case-by-case and either placed together or separated based on their needs. Fortunately these days many more school districts are getting on the bandwagon and educating themselves on the particular requirements of multiples, not only how their emotional and social development differs from that of single-born children, but also how it affects their educational progress.

The Twin Bond and Socialization

Many believe that the close nature of the twin relationship (and that among triplets and quads) can hinder their social development, particularly during the school years when most children begin to make friends outside of the family unit. Those who align themselves with this point of view feel that if twins are allowed to be together in the same classroom they will isolate themselves, choosing to play with just each other rather than with their fellow classmates. While some multiples may cling solely to each other, many interact successfully with their classmates and teachers. Research shows that multiples across all six subgroups network with a variety of playmates other than their cotwins. Many do, however, feel more comfortable in reaching out to others when their cotwin is nearby (in the same classroom). In fact, girls from same-sex pairs actually seem more social toward their classmates when they are in the same classroom—their twin status draws attention to them, making them more approachable in the eyes of other classmates. Their fellow students may deliberately seek the pair out, perhaps

> **From One Parent to Another**
>
> "We chose to have Troy and Alissa (DZOS) in the same class. They have been together in the same classroom since preschool, and they are in the third grade right now. They will remain together until they ask to be separated or until they reach middle school or high school age and take different classes."

seeing them as special and more interesting than single-born children.

With that said, however, many twins do enjoy working together rather than independently. Therefore, parents and teachers should encourage twins in the same classroom to sit at separate tables and partner with a variety of children. It should never be assumed that since twins are together they should collaborate on every project or task.

Does Classroom Separation Encourage Individuality?

In one study done in Australia, researchers asked more than one thousand teachers what they thought was the most important reason for classroom separation; more than 90 percent indicated that it's better for individual development. Yet the researchers of the study stressed that there's no empirical evidence—other than with the most severe pathological cases—to back up this belief. On the other hand, there are some researchers who do believe that classroom separation is advan-

---

From One Parent to Another

"I remember one year we asked that the boys be assigned to different teachers because we felt that Dan (DZSSm) would relate really well with the male teacher who liked to toss the football around on the playground with his students while Todd (DZSSm) would flourish under the teacher who had a reputation for providing individualized, challenging assignments to accommodate higher learners. Two years later, we requested that the boys be placed together in a classroom because of the positive experience we had with the particular teacher with our older son. We also felt that Todd and Dan would benefit from being their own learning team. It was interesting to walk past their bedroom after they had gone to bed and the lights were out and hear them discussing a book they were reading in school. Being together in class did backfire on us once, however. Todd had spent a lot of time working on a class assignment. Dan forgot about the assignment until the last minute, so he copied most of Todd's! The next morning, Todd discovered what Dan had done, so he hastily redid his. Dan got an A and Todd got an A– on the assignment. We had a long talk with Dan about doing his own work, and it never happened again."

---

tageous, believing that twins who are in separate classrooms are forced to cooperate with their classmates and work independently, thereby lessening the pair's intradependence and strengthening each child's sense of identity. In addition, they say that classroom separation eliminates the temptation to compare twins or relate to them as one entity—fellow students and the teacher perceive and assess each twin based on his "own individual merits. Yet these same researchers admit there is little or no difference in individuation between same- and parallel-class twins and speculate that perhaps the pair does not take full advantage of their separation, viewing it instead as a punishment. In other words, the jury is still out on the issue of whether classroom separation encourages individuality.

Whatever your belief, it's important to remember that school is a small portion of a child's life and what goes on the other eighteen hours a day when twins are not in school matters more—things like parental attitudes and behavior, sibling relationships, participation in other group activities, and so forth.

Is It Better to Separate Sooner Rather than Later?

Since young children are quite adaptable, the best time to separate twins is when they first start school, right? Not necessarily. Many researchers question the logic behind early separation, especially when it comes to MZ twins who are innately similar and more tightly bonded than any other twin subgroup. Not only is adjusting to kindergarten difficult, they argue, but having to adapt to classroom life without the person who has been so strongly tied to their own young life seems almost cruel. On the other hand, some researchers argue that early separation is an important part of preparing for the inevitable separation of adulthood. The earlier, they say, the greater the chance for a child to adapt to change.

Although there has been very little research in the past on the behavior of twins who were separated early versus those who were kept together, more studies are popping up. For instance, a longitudinal study done in the United Kingdom in 2004 looked at whether classroom separation had any effect on behavior, school progress, and reading abilities—as reported by the child's teacher—on seven-year-old, identical and same-sex nonidentical twins, and whether it varied by zygosity. Several important results stand out: twins who were separated in the first year of school had more internalizing problems (self-esteem issues, anxiety, and depression) than those who were not separated. MZ twins' troubles actually escalated in the first year following separation. They also found that those who were separated had more reading problems than those who were not separated, with young MZ twins once again topping the list.

Yet, it wasn't all bad news for separated twins. In fact, the UK study found that DZ twins who were separated after the first year were much harder working than those who stayed together. Another more in-depth study done in the Netherlands a year later replicated the UK study but this time took into account the parents' observations (in addition to the teachers') and preexisting problems before separation, and followed both the short- and long-term effects of separation. Their conclusions were similar to the first study: in the short-term, separated MZ as well as DZ seven-year-old twins showed more internalizing problems than nonseparated twins. In the long term, when corrected for preexisting conditions, twelve-year-old twins had no additional long-term effect. There was also no difference in academic achievement between older separated and nonseparated twins.

Although these studies indicate that early separation may cause emotional trauma for some young children, remember it's not the case for all. Neither study took into account the child's point of view—whether or not he wants to share the classroom spotlight with his cotwin—or the case for autonomy and if separation actually helps in developing individual identity. And remember, too, these studies were done overseas and may have a cultural bias. In other words, what doesn't work in the United Kingdom and the Netherlands may in fact work in the United States, and vice versa. Flexibility and open communication between parents and school administrators in assessing each set of twins individually is once again the key to school success.

A few parents told me that when their children were forced to separate, they suffered either behaviorally or academically, but when reunited in the same classroom the following year, the problems dissipated. For instance, one mom whose DZ (nonidentical) sons were separated in first grade had a dismal year—one son didn't connect with his fellow classmates and therefore had trouble concentrating on his work. Unfortunately, the school principal refused to put the boys together the following year even at their mother's insistence. Several meetings later, including one with the regional superintendent, the boys were allowed to attend the same classroom. There they each had an exceptional year. It's hard to say whether the success is attributed to their being in the same class or being one year older.

Making the Decision

When it came to the issue of classroom separation, the parents I interviewed for this book were split right down the middle—half chose to have their multiples in the same kindergarten class while the other half decided to separate them. Most of the parents who kept their children together said there was no reason not to—their multiples got along well with each other and their fellow classmates, cooperated rather than competed, and just genuinely enjoyed being together. (However, a few reluctantly put them together as their schools had only one kindergarten class.) Still, nearly half of this former group separated their multiples in first grade stating that "it was time."

On the other hand, the reasons for parents' decisions to separate their multiples varied somewhat. Several said they "just knew" it would work out better, while others felt differences in learning styles and abilities warranted a bit of space between the pair. One family requested that their daughters remain together but "lost the battle." Interestingly, nine sets of MZ twins began their school careers in separate classrooms, their parents sensing that constantly being confused for their cotwin in preschool got old quickly for the pair. Several identical twins actually asked their parents to be separated.

Following is a set of guidelines and questions to help you make your decision. To make the best choice for your multiples, we'll address the issue open-endedly rather than taking a for or against stance. This will allow parents to think about classroom separation from many angles, to consider the whole child rather than just one perspective, and then to choose the best solution. Keep in mind, too, that a child may dominate at home but become much more passive in school, so before deciding observe your multiples in various situations such as play and quiet activities. It's important, too, for parents to step back and try to evaluate the situation constructively rather than emotionally. And finally, parents should get opinions and feedback from their multiples' preschool teachers and other professionals who have come into contact with their children—their opinions are not only valuable but may be different from what parents have observed in their children.

Ability. Is one twin markedly more able than the other? Does the less-able multiple continually opt out of activities in which she struggles while her cotwin excels? Does one see herself as failing or less than her twin, or does the more able one deliberately hold back in order to stay on track with his sibling? Does the more-able twin do the work for the less-able twin? (While on the surface it may seem useful or even sweet that one twin helps the other with her schoolwork, over time you may find that it creates uncomfortable roles for each child.) Or, does the pair "specialize," where one masters reading, for instance, convincing the other that now she doesn't need to?

Differing ability was the number one reason overall parents gave for choosing to separate their twins. And with good reason: allowing each multiple the opportunity to learn at his own speed and in his own way without trying to keep pace with a cotwin is beneficial to both children.

Behavior. Are your twins constantly trying to outdo the other? (If twins are competitive at school and not at home, other reasons could be at play here—perhaps classmates encourage the pair to go against each other.) Are they disruptive in class, banding together to dominate; do they continually fight with each other or deliberately disturb classmates, the teacher, or even each other? Do they compete for the teacher's attention? Is tattling an issue, where one or both report back to the parents the wrongdoings of the other? Although separation usually stops the pair from fighting with each other in the classroom, it may not change either's disruptive behavior (they could each easily band together with other willing children in their separate classrooms and continue to wreak havoc), and other intervention may be necessary.

Their Bond. Do the children have a strong fear of being separated? (If so, parents and teachers need to acknowledge the fear as real in order to eventually help each twin discover that he can in fact stand on his own two feet.) Are they codependent, where one or both cannot comfortably socialize with other children? In other words, do they feel incomplete or only half of a whole? Although separate classrooms allow each child to discover that she can in fact function very well on her own, it may prove to be too stressful for the pair during the early elementary years.

Does one twin continually dominate or restrict the other? For instance, does one twin speak for the other, never allowing the quieter twin to answer; boss her cotwin, directing him in play; or in the case of opposite-sex twins, does the female "overmother" the male twin, often completing simple life-skill tasks for him such as tying his shoes? When the "passive" child is placed in a separate class, he or she often blossoms, his or her self-esteem growing in the process, while the "dominant" child often has a harder time adjusting to the classroom without his or her cotwin. If your twins are identical, would they feel frustrated if their teacher or fellow students mixed them up in class?

Socialization. Do they enjoy being around other children? Do they make friends easily? Have they spent any time away from each other, perhaps visiting Grandma's house alone, or attended different days of preschool? Do they enjoy spending time alone? Outgoing and socially mature children usually adjust well in either scenario.

Speech and Language. Are one or both twins struggling with speech, or does one twin speak for the other twin? Often separate classrooms give each multiple a greater opportunity to practice his verbal skills on his own.

Family Life. Have the twins recently experienced a loss such as the death of a parent or sibling, or has there been a divorce in the family where the support of a cotwin would be valuable? Has the family recently moved to a new state or new school district where having a classroom ally would enable each to concentrate better while adjusting?

How Others View Your Twins. Is the pair constantly compared to one another? Do

---

From One Parent to Another

"Like many parents we hemmed and hawed when it came time to make the decision about splitting up in school. Ultimately we decided to keep them together for kindergarten, and among the many reasons on both sides, we thought what is the harm in nurturing that twin bond one more year if they do get along and they do function reasonably well together? When Rachel and Nicole (MZf) started first grade, it wasn't really a question for us, we just knew it was time. Not because of anything their kindergarten teacher said, but we knew they needed a little more independence; we could tell they were getting weary of people not knowing who was who."

other children relate to them as one and the same? For instance, do children group their names together? Have peers labeled each child, such as "the quiet one" or "the smart one"? Some twins won't be bothered by how their classmates view them; other multiples will and may request separate classrooms.

Seeing It from Both Sides

My twins are in a somewhat unique situation—they began preschool together, were separated from kindergarten through third grade, and now in fourth grade share the same classroom once again. I won't weigh in on individuality/autonomy issues, but rather I'll illuminate what I think are more basic observations to both classroom scenarios.

> ### From One Parent to Another
>
> "We had Gabriel and Jordan (MZm) together for the first couple of years of preschool—we felt that it was important that they have each other. We finally separated them after the kids in their class weren't distinguishing between them. They would come up to them and say, 'Which one are you, Gabriel or Jordan?' It was getting in the way of their having individual friendships. They were at different developmental levels, too. Plus, sometimes Gabriel was dominating—Jordan would follow him around. They did very well with the separation."

Before my sons entered preschool, they had never spent much time apart, and since school was a completely new experience for them, I naturally put them together in the same classroom. It worked well for a while, but by the middle of the second year, I noticed little signs indicating that maybe it was time for a change. For instance, when one boy brought in the class snack, the children politely thanked both boys instead of the one whose turn it was. This was upsetting to him. He told me he wanted them to thank just him and not his brother. He couldn't articulate exactly why that upset him, but it was clear to me—he didn't want to be automatically lumped together with his twin. He wanted his classmates to see him for himself.

There were other signs, too. If something interesting or exciting happened in the classroom that day, it was a race home to see who'd be the first one to tell me. There were always tears from the boy who didn't get to me in time. And finally, if one boy wasn't cooperative that day and was reprimanded by his teachers, the other twin tried coming to his rescue. It was always the same twin who wouldn't cooperate, and I feared that the teachers were quietly labeling them the good twin and the bad twin. Small signals such as these brought us to the ultimate decision to separate them in kindergarten the following year.

After four years of them being in separate classrooms, I can expand on the positive attributes. For starters, and most important, it allowed each child to have his own separate school experiences that he could proudly share with all of us every evening at the dinner table. It's my belief that unique, solitary events—a moment that each child can call his very own—are things that many twins sadly lack. Their circle of friends is wider too, each sharing his classroom buddies with the other. By being in separate classes, they simply know more kids. My circle of knowledge and community is larger as well. I'm connected with more parents and teachers than if they had been placed together all these years.

I've heard the complaint that when kids are separated, they tend to have different amounts of homework, class projects, field trips, and so on, causing chaos in the home and bad feelings between the twins when one needs to spend more time on schoolwork than the other. It's absolutely true. When you have same-grade children in different classes, you'll hear a lot of grumbling: "It's not fair! Why did he get ten minutes of homework while I got an hour?" But I've used these objections as a teaching tool—I tell my kids all the time that someone will always have more homework, go on the "cooler" class trip, have the nicer teacher, or get the easier class project. That's life. Life isn't always fair. Hopefully they're absorbing these simple life lessons that will help them to cope with much more difficult problems they are sure to encounter in the future.

For fourth grade we chose to have them in the same class for no other reason than the teacher—she was highly recommended. (A few parents I interviewed also put their multiples in the same class at one time based on a teacher's positive reputation.) And yes, life is now easier—they can study for tests together, help each other if one gets stuck on a homework problem, and I don't have to split my time volunteering for both their classrooms. And yes, they're both enjoying the experience very much (they are best friends, after all). They seem very relaxed with each other in the same classroom. According to their teacher, there's no rivalry between the two. Yet now we're dealing with other issues. Although we have a "no tattle" rule, it took only five days of school for someone to break it. Obviously, it's one twin challenge that we need to work on. And once again, just as in preschool, nearly every day there's a

> ### From One Parent to Another
>
> "They were in the same class until fourth grade. It was easier for me. I wanted them to have the same assignments at the same time. But Jeffrey (DZSSm) was so scattered and would lose his homework a lot of the time. I'd have to make a copy of Andrew's so that Jeffrey could do his. That used to make Andrew furious. He'd say, 'Why does Jeffrey have to get mine? Why can't he keep up with his own stuff?' Jeffrey just didn't pay attention to things. Probably because he knew that Andrew would have it. Now in high school they have a few classes together and Jeffrey still asks Andrew for the homework, only now it doesn't seem to bother Andrew as much."

From One Parent to Another

"Amber and Cortney (DZSSf) were in the same class until third grade when Cortney decided she wanted them to be in different classes. I think it actually helped them since before they were together all the time. They were together from the morning when I dropped them off to when I picked them up from the extended learning program at night. It was a lot of togetherness—they'd end up arguing and bickering. I noticed that when they were in different classes, they were very nice to each other since they had a lot more to talk about."

---

fight to see who can get to me first to tell me all about the day's events.

So what will we do for next year? After much thought, we decided to separate them again for the sole reason that they spend 24-7 together and a little space between them, even if it's only a classroom away, would benefit both boys. Additionally, I'm noticing that their friends are beginning to group them together rather than seeking out each boy individually. Separate classrooms will help them cultivate a few separate friendships.

If Separation Is on the Horizon

If classroom separation seems like the right choice for your multiples, start preparing them well before the first day of school. Even some outgoing and happy-go-lucky twins will find the transition difficult to make. After all, they've spent nearly every waking moment together since birth. Therefore, it's imperative that parents start the weaning process well before the first bell.

- Take each child on separate outings regularly. Begin with slow, gradual separation such as a quick trip to the store and build up the time away from each other to an afternoon with just the two of you.

- Openly talk about the upcoming separation. Focus on the positive. Role-play or tell stories to help each child imagine what his school experiences will be like without his cotwin.
- Speak with school administrators about allowing the twins to "check in" with each other during the day if they so desire.
- Encourage outside friendships by arranging double play-dates both at your own home and perhaps an occasional separate playdate at other children's homes.
- Let each child explore his interests at will, and don't insist on constant twin togetherness.
- Give each child time to adjust to school life sans cotwin. If the going gets tough, offer support and encouragement rather than quickly reversing the situation. Most twins just need time.

Reassess Placement Yearly

School separation shouldn't be viewed as an either/or issue—either we separate them or we don't—but rather as an ongoing process. It's important for parents to keep an open mind and revisit their decision every year. I was amazed at the number of parents I surveyed whose children "hopped" from year to year—separated one year, together the next. Each spring set up an appointment with your children's teachers to get their opinion. Observe your twins in the classroom and keep tabs on their achievements and struggles. This year perhaps your children should be placed in the same class, but who knows what their situation will warrant next year. If, for instance, your twins are together this year and one is struggling while the other is excelling, hurting the struggling twin's self-esteem, maybe you should reconsider their placement for next year.

The Triplet Conundrum

You think you have it rough trying to figure out whether to separate your twins? Just imagine if you had triplets! Since many triplets consist of a set of identical (MZ) twins with a third nonidentical sibling (DZ), the problem of school separation is compounded. Many small school districts don't have enough same-grade classes for a three-way split. Yet separating the fraternal (DZ) child from her identical (MZ) sisters would have possible devastating effects, as the dizygotic child would feel completely left out. In cases such as this, the best solution would be to place all three together but allow them some sense of privacy and individuality by seating them at separate tables. If this is the plan, and to compensate for their constant togetherness, parents of triplets may want to consider enrolling each child in a separate after-school activity or sport.

Being an Advocate for Your Multiples

Why is it that parents with twins, triplets, and quads seem to disagree with school administrators more frequently than parents with single-born children? The conflicts can range from something as simple (but frustrating) as straightening out a mix-up between your twins' school reports to something as embittered as struggling to keep your multiples together in the same classroom. To be fair, not all school districts are difficult and not all parents will need to do battle. Many school officials are open to the opinions and concerns of parents with multiples and pay attention to the specific educational needs of multiples. In fact, only four families out of the forty-four I surveyed spoke of stubborn administrators. Still many families clash yearly with their school districts when it comes to keeping their children together or simply getting their kids the services they need.

The number one challenge for both parents and educators is the classroom separation issue—some schools feel that separating multiples is best, while some parents prefer to keep their kids together, at least until there's sufficient evidence that warrants a separation. From the school's point of view it comes from the belief that twins will have an easier time individuating—developing personal autonomy—if they are put into separate classes. Another worry is the issue of equality. A survey of 584 Australian teachers, for instance, cited fairness as a concern when it comes to having twins in the same classroom. Many said it was just too easy to compare the two or that they felt pressure to keep the pair at the same academic level.

So how can parents help educators understand the true nature of the twin relationship and how it affects their learning? Better communication is needed among school officials, teachers, and parents of multiples. One mom told me that since they're a military family that has lived in seven different states in twelve years, keeping their children (DZSSf) together in the same classroom was important. To accomplish their goal, they took a proactive as well as preemptive approach. As soon as they arrived in a new school district, for instance, they sent a letter to the principal requesting that their girls stay together and included supporting information such as published studies on the subject as well as a letter of recommendation from the girls' past teachers attesting to how well they did in the same classroom.

If you anticipate trouble with keeping your twins together, here are a few other ideas to help you fight the battle.

- Well before kindergarten enrollment begins, find out what your district's written policy is on multiples in the classroom. Call the school or the district office directly. If the district doesn't have a written policy, that's one point in your favor when it comes to keeping your twins together if you so choose, but that doesn't mean the school's principal won't have a strong opinion against it.

- If your school has an "unofficial policy" of separating all multiples, that's where a face-to-face conference with your school principal is in order. Attend the meeting prepared with documents that back up the claim that keeping twins together does not hinder their individuation (check out the back of this book for the appropriate studies or contact the National Organization of Mothers of Twins Clubs for documentation) and that sometimes identical twins have a difficult time in separate classes because of their intrinsically tight bond. Calmly listen and address the principal's concerns. Often a meeting is enough to convince him or her that your twins should at least be able to be assigned to the same classroom on a trial basis.

- If you hit a dead end or your district's written policy has a strict clause stating that all multiples will be separated, your next step is to write a letter to the superintendent of your district (send it by registered mail, and always follow up with a phone call several days later once the letter has been received) or attend your local school board meeting and voice your opinion for change. Contact your local Mothers of Twins Club and rally support from other parents of multiples through a letter and e-mail writing campaign.

- If you've exhausted all avenues and are still not getting anywhere, your choices for the next step are to enroll your children in a private, charter, or magnet school that would accommodate your wishes; hire an attorney and prepare to do battle; or do as one Minnesota mom did in 2005 and lobby to change the state law. This courageous mom, a legislative aide for a state senator, helped to draft legislation stating that parents should have the final say in classroom placement of multiples. The bill passed both Minnesota's House and Senate unanimously and is the first law of its kind in the United States. Parents in Texas, Illinois, North Carolina, New York, and Massachusetts are also banding together to push through similar legislation. Log on to the Nationwide Campaign for Twin Bill Legislation at twinslegislation.com for an update on which states are fighting the battle for their kids.

WHEN MULTIPLES DIFFER IN ABILITY

Not long ago I received a letter from our school district asking to test one of my twins for possible inclusion in the gifted program. My initial reaction of pride was tempered with, "Why not the other, too? He's just as smart!" I was shocked at my reaction and had to take a step back to think about all its implications. Although I was happy and proud of my achieving twin, my

Homework Helpers

Should you allow your multiples to help each other with their homework? Sounds tempting, especially if you're clueless like me when it comes to math! Will they actually tutor each other, or will they just give each other the answers, taking the easy way out instead? And if you let them make a habit of it, will they approach all their work as a group effort rather than each exploring a subject at his own pace?

Many educators believe that peer learning, the process in which one student with a strong grasp of a subject explains what he knows in a language that's understandable to a fellow struggling student, is beneficial. And some experts point out that when one twin helps his cotwin with his

(continued on next page)

Homework Helpers *(continued)*

schoolwork it actually diminishes competition, as the helper feels proud when his "student" excels and receives a high grade.

Before diving in, though, make sure the "teacher" actually wants to help (he may feel burdened by the task) and the "student" wants the assistance (he may be threatened by his cotwin's knowledge). If either is the case, a hired tutor may be your answer instead. Also, try to have your twins help each other in a public room such as the kitchen or den so you can keep an eye on the proceedings to make sure one is actually helping rather than offering the other a homework freebie.

thoughts couldn't leave the one left behind. Was that fair? My reaction isn't atypical for parents with multiples. Issues of differing academic abilities are common, leaving many parents feeling confused about what to do. But the reality is that it's usually more of a problem for the parents than the twins themselves, and unfortunately, it's frequently poor handling of the situation that sticks with the twins long after they've grown rather than the disappointment of not achieving the same goal as a cotwin.

Should You Let One Twin Skip a Grade?

Do you have a budding math genius? Or do you live with the next great American novelist? For every twin who struggles with reading, there are plenty of multiples out there far exceeding their grade-level potential, prompting many parents to ask, "Should we let him skip a grade?" Yet before you bump your prodigy up a year, you need to carefully consider several issues such as maturity, his bond with his cotwin, as well as what's in his best interest both in the short and long term.

First of all, while skipping a grade may be a good academic fit this year, what about next year? Often children are only temporarily bored with reading or math at their current grade level as it quickly heats up the following year. And while it's great to offer more challenging work, it may not be beneficial to push too soon. Next, you need to think about your child's physical and social maturity. Once again, his immaturity and small stature may not be a problem in lower grades, but once puberty hits and the gap widens it could cause serious socialization problems for your child. And finally, you need to think about the implications of skipping a grade on the cotwin. Will one twin forever be in the shadow of her cotwin if one skips a grade?

Before proceeding, you may want to pull your high-achieving multiple aside to get her reaction separately and privately. Does she want to leave her current grade and her cotwin? If not, there are other ways to offer intellectual stimulation than just moving ahead a grade. Look for a challenging after-school enrichment program, such as

---

From One Parent to Another

"Todd (DZSSm) qualified for a gifted program in elementary school and was in the honors track in middle school and high school. This definitely required a delicate balancing act and was probably our biggest challenge during the school years. We didn't want to make Dan (DZSSm) feel like he was not as good as his brother, yet we also didn't want to downplay Todd's accomplishments. At first, I think this was hard for Dan, especially when insensitive classmates in elementary school would say, 'You aren't as smart as Todd.' As time went on, Dan just came to accept that Todd is smart. In contrast, Dan is very socially adept. He's a happy young man who is doing fine as a business major in college. In turn, Todd learned that being smart is not the only thing that defines a person. He never brags or acts superior; he is a quiet leader who is willing to give credit to others."

chess or math club, or investigate art or music lessons. Or see if your child's teacher can provide additional projects or if the school can arrange to have your young Einstein move up to a higher grade for only part of the day, say for math or reading, enabling her to spend the majority of the day with her current classmates and, more important, her cotwin.

Should You Hold One Struggling Twin Back?

You've watched one of your twins profoundly struggle with school and you can't help but ask yourself, "Should I hold him back?" It's the ultimate painful question for some parents of multiples and should be carefully considered before going forward and irrevocably changing the course of your multiples' educational careers.

First, get a proper diagnosis for the struggling twin from an education specialist or psychologist. Only then will you find out if he's merely struggling in one area or has deeper disabilities. And if he has a disability, is it long-term or can it be successfully remediated?

There's strong evidence, too, that suggests that grade retention simply doesn't work as simply repeating a subject you found confusing probably won't help you comprehend it any better. It's more important to know why you didn't understand the subject in the first place.

And finally, the struggling twin's personality must be considered also. How will being held back affect his self-esteem and his bond to his cotwin? Nothing calls attention to the differences between twins more than when one repeats a grade. If retention is the only solution, strongly consider transferring the struggling twin to a different school so he'll be out of range of unwanted comparisons. The more able twin would benefit, too, by relieving her guilt from outperforming her cotwin.

Another option is to home-school the struggling twin to give him the help and attention he needs until he can be main-streamed back into the same grade as his twin.

Several parents told me of their internal debate surrounding retaining one or both of their twins. Parents of a set of DZSSf, for instance, ultimately made the decision to hold one of their daughters back. "It was a difficult decision," the mom admitted. "She's struggling academically in school, especially in reading where she's a full grade behind, although she tries very hard. She's also socially immature and can't relate well to her peers. I don't want her to lose her enthusiasm for school and learning and just give up because everything is too hard."

From One Parent to Another

"In his junior year Michael (DZOSm) failed all of his academic subjects. He tried to cram it all in night school and summer school, which was impossible, and in senior year he was not ready for those subjects. He was left back and had to repeat his senior year. Both he and Victoria (DZOSf) were devastated that they did not graduate together. At graduation, she cried in her seat, he cried in the balcony. My heart broke for both of them."

Special Consideration for Opposite-Sex Twins

When it comes to school and boy-girl twins, a few obstacles can surface. First of all, research indicates that twin boys, on average, lag behind girls academically in the primary school years. So if a female twin outperforms her brother scholastically, should a parent consider school separation? Yes, and with good reason. The male twin's self-esteem may further drop as he struggles to keep pace with a sister who continues to excel. To make matters worse, he may opt or tune out thinking there is no reason to try any harder since she has it all wrapped up.

From One Parent to Another

"Our reason for separating them was because of her mothering and dominating him all the time and him just letting her do it. I felt he needed an opportunity to be on his own and build on his self-esteem and independence. I wanted Kyle (DZOSm) to know that he could function without his sister around all the time. I also wanted Carissa (DZOSf) to learn that not every little friend would let her be the boss all the time and that she needed to learn how to allow someone else to be the leader."

Another point to consider is the socialization issue. In Chapter 1, we discussed how the female in opposite-sex twins tend to "overmother" (some might even suggest "boss") their brothers. In the days prior to school, some boys actually like when their sisters take the initiative. Who wouldn't want someone to tie his shoes or help him pour a glass of juice? Yet by the time they reach school, the boys on the receiving end of this constant aid usually no longer like it. As they begin to explore the outside world, they find their sisters' actions intrusive. Yet it's often difficult to change their behavior as the roles have been set for several years. Or, in the case where the boys are still dependent on their sisters, some of the girls don't appreciate having to rescue their brothers much either. Many girls don't like being forced into becoming the dominant partner.

How Parents Can Help

When two single-born children perform differently at school, most parents take it in stride—they're different people. Yet when you have multiples whose school careers are parallel, their imbalances are magnified. Help your multiples understand and appreciate their differences by following these tips.

- Keep an ongoing dialogue about how everyone in life is different. Although they're twins, they're also different people. Let them get used to the idea that each will be better at different things.

- If competition and comparisons heat up and are ongoing, consider ways in which they have fewer opportunities to be compared. Perhaps they'd like to play different sports (or different positions within the same sport) or pursue different activities. If that doesn't work and the comparisons are in the way of sibling harmony, you may consider having them attend different schools.

- Step in before the girl-boy balance shifts unevenly and permanent, unhealthy roles are established. Encourage both to be independent and do for themselves.

- From an early age, offer each his or her own room or at least adequate privacy where each child is allowed to explore his or her own interests at will.

- Consider classroom separation for opposite-sex twins, especially if the female is more advanced academically than her male cotwin.

- Don't make your twin's weaknesses be your sole focus with little consideration for his strengths. Work on building the struggling twin's performance in school and congratulate his achievements. But don't forget the more able twin. If no congratulations come her way, she'll quickly think that nothing she does is worth much. Never overlook one twin's achievements for the sake of sparing the other's feelings.

LEARNING DIFFICULTIES

Another pressing question when it comes to multiples and education is whether they experience more learning problems than single-born children. The answer quite simply is yes, but the reasons why are not as clear. As was mentioned earlier in this chapter, preschool language difficulties impact a twin's ability to read later on in grade school. Furthermore, twin boys struggle more than twin girls, but the reasons for the discrepancy between the sexes is still not completely understood.

The good news, however, is that being a multiple doesn't necessarily mean children will struggle in school or, even if they do, that they are any less intelligent. In fact, the La Trobe Twin Study found that many of the twins who struggled learning to read tested above average in nonreading skills. Furthermore, in a recent Dutch study, researchers concluded that there is no difference in cognitive performance between twins and their nontwin siblings. So clearly intelligence is not the issue here. The purpose of calling attention to the problems some multiples have is so that parents can turn up the antenna and tune in to their multiples' individual educational needs. If a problem is caught early (most disabilities are evident within the first few years of childhood) and then successfully remedied, there's no limit to a twin's achievements.

Do Boys and Girls Learn Differently?

If you've ever stepped inside any second grade classroom you've seen something interesting—most of the boys are fidgeting in their seats, eyes fixed on the world outside their classroom windows, while most of the little girls have their noses in their books, dutifully learning their lessons. Why is that? It's part biology and part sociology. Simply stated—males are wired differently than females. All this translates to young girls being better classroom students than boys. Although girls may achieve better grades than boys in the early years, however, most boys catch up scholastically to their female classmates by the time they reach the teen years. And while twin girls struggle a bit behind single-born girls, they too catch up by high school. Unfortunately for some twin boys, the problems holding them behind both single-born children and twin girls may persist even longer. By age fourteen, for instance, one study found that only 42 percent of twin boys had reached adequate standards of literacy compared with 71 percent of singleton boys.

Although much more investigation is needed to understand why, one thing is apparent—reading problems in twin boys are linked with preschool language difficulties. The La Trobe Twin Study, for example, found that preschool twin boys who experienced two out of the seven common language difficulties almost always faced significant reading problems later—both in reading accuracy and comprehension. Compounding the situation is twin boys' high level of distraction; those who struggled with reading also had difficulty concentrating and were more careless in their work. Less able to focus on their schoolwork for any length of time, many twin boys are quickly labeled hyperactive. Researchers speculate that perhaps since early childhood twin boys rarely had the opportunity to do any task without the interruption of their cotwin or always competed to be the first one done—concentrating more on finishing first than on the quality of the work. Lessons in prioritizing their work, developing routines, and staying on task can help alleviate the condition and ultimately improve their level of academic success.

How Parents Can Help

Children perform better in school when parents take an active role in their academic lives. The best time to combat learning difficulties is as soon as they're diagnosed, but even if you've just realized your grade-school twin is struggling, it's never too late to get help. Listed below are a few ideas to incorporate into your daily family routine.

- Have your children read to you nightly and emphasize word accuracy by helping them sound out syllables phonetically. Research has shown that the continual and consistent process of reading helps the brain make linguistic connections.

- Try reading with each twin separately and privately so as not to create a competition between the pair, especially if one twin is a more advanced reader. Accuracy, not speed, is most important. In addition, each needs time to discern the material and ask questions independent of his cotwin.

- Follow a nightly homework routine—designate a quiet, clutter-free place to do work and enforce quiet time so that multiples can concentrate more easily on school-related tasks. Stress the need for carefully produced work, and discourage one twin from rushing to finish his work before his cotwin does.

- Movement actually helps boys to learn—it stimulates their brains and calms their impulsive behavior. If a boy acts impetuously in class, the use of a squeeze-ball can help channel some of that energy. More physical movement in the classroom such as aiding the teacher in handing out assignments or an hourly stretch can help too.

- Keep an ongoing dialogue with your twins' teachers about their progress and problems. Inform them of any special tutoring you've scheduled for your children.

- If home-care isn't helping, schedule an assessment with the school psychologist to get a handle on your child's strengths and weaknesses. You need to know specifically what the problem is so that you can seek accurate remediation.

- Although getting the help that struggling readers need is paramount, it's not their entire school career. Don't make it the sole focus—offer encouragement on other school subjects in which they shine as well.

Attention-Deficit/Hyperactivity Disorder

We've heard a lot about attention-deficit/hyperactivity disorder (ADHD) lately in the news, but what exactly is it? ADHD is a developmental disorder that manifests itself in childhood. Inattention, impulsiveness, and hyperactivity are the three components of ADHD. Within that definition are three subtypes of the disorder—the most common form affects those with mostly inattentive symptoms (kids seem to daydream, not pay attention or stay on task easily); the second affects children who exhibit mostly hyperactivity and impulsiveness (these are the fidgety kids who often act on impulse); and finally, the third affects those with a combination of these symptoms. It is interesting to note that kids who have any form of ADHD can concentrate on a task as long as it is something that holds their interest such as a favorite movie or video game. Problems occur, however, when that attention is redirected to something that does not.

Although these days there are many who question the existence of ADHD, it's a real disorder recognized by the medical community and has been identified since the early twentieth century. In the initial days, however, it was called a variety of different names such as "restlessness syndrome." Therefore, ADHD may seem like a new fad for Generation X, but it's not. In fact, ADHD is just as prevalent in other countries as it is here in the United States; therefore the frenetic pace of American culture is not to blame.

And why does a discussion of ADHD come into play in a book on twins and higher-order multiples? This highly heritable disorder is unfortunately more common in twins than single-born children. To break it down further still, twin boys experience more behavioral problems than twin girls (the inattentive type is the most common in twin boys, the hyperactive form is the rarest), and since ADHD has a strong genetic component, if one MZ twin is diagnosed with a form of ADHD, the other twin has a much higher incidence of it, too. The problem for multiples is compounded for twin boys because they often exhibit inattention without hyperactivity, resulting in fewer accurate diagnoses. Yet a child who's inattentive often suffers in school and doesn't perform up to his potential. Furthermore, there's a high rate of comorbidity with ADHD—twins who exhibit either the inattentive type or combined type of ADHD also experience a higher degree of learning problems in both speech and reading. If left untreated, children with ADHD grow up to be adolescents with ADHD and are more inclined to indulge in risk-taking behavior such as underage drinking, drug abuse, delinquency, and even sexual promiscuity.

The child with ADHD can wreak havoc and put undue stress on the family dynamics as well—in particular the condition can adversely affect the twinship. Non-ADHD twins often feel anxious and report a high degree of conflict within the relationship with their cotwins who have the disorder.

Fortunately, ADHD is treatable either through medication alone or a combination of medication and behavioral/psychological treatment, but a proper diagnosis is paramount. On the home front, parents can help their multiples with inattentive and impulsive behavior by gently reminding their twins to slow down. They should also encourage twins to finish tasks and to focus on the quality of the work rather than the speed with which it is completed. Speak with your child's teacher, too, about ways to make the classroom environment more amenable to concentration such as moving his desk closer to the teacher, breaking down larger assignments into several smaller sections, and offering verbal reminders of what's expected more often.

> ### From One Parent to Another
>
> "Christina (DZOSf) had trouble reading and was later diagnosed with ADD. Before the diagnosis, things were tough because her brother (DZOSm) was a much better reader and got better grades. Her self-esteem dropped very low. She even played dumb when she knew the answer, since it was easier playing dumb than chancing getting something wrong. Their relationship was still strong, but she was feeling badly about herself. After the diagnosis and when she started taking medication, her entire learning ability changed. She has been on the honor roll ever since and feels much better about herself."

SCHOOL IS NOW IN SESSION

From kindergarten readiness to the hotly debated classroom separation issue, from differing abilities to disabilities, the subject of twins and education is jam-packed with questions and decisions. A few things are a given, however—multiples need a little extra attention and understanding to ensure that their experiences are up to par with their single-born contemporaries. Ultimately, it's the positive attitude of parents and the flexibility in policy of educators that can make the difference between school success or stress.

5

Combating Competition and
Promoting Cooperation

Making comparisons among children is normal in all families—nearly every parent does it. It usually begins early and
somewhat innocently ("My oldest daughter was such a good
sleeper, but my youngest is the worst!"). I'm sure you remember doing it when your multiples were babies. You'd stare lovingly at them while they peacefully slept, and like most
parents, you began to notice little similarities ("Oh, look!
They both have a dimple in their chins.") or subtle differences
("His hair is so curly, while hers is so straight."). It was impossible not to compare them since they were side by side 24-7.
Parents with MZ (identical) twins searched for what was different about the pair, while those with DZ (fraternal) multiples
looked for similarities. And what about the grandparents and
the next-door neighbors? They did it, too. Perhaps a little too
much sometimes ("Why is he always crying, while she's such a
good baby?").

There's really no harm in comparing twins during this early
stage of life. (After all, they have no idea what you're saying.)

But trouble can lurk right around the corner if it persists as your multiples get older, especially if your twins continue to pursue the same interests as some like to do. This constant comparing and contrasting of twins can lead to a rivalrous relationship. While encouraging each to find her own unique calling may help build cooperation, it's not a complete solution. Nor should you insist that your multiples take up different interests, especially if they share the same enthusiasm for a hobby or sport as many identical twins often do. (Could you imagine, for instance, flipping a coin to see who gets to learn to play the piano when both show a desire?) Instead it's the parents' attitudes—whether they view and treat their children as individuals or as a joint entity—and how they protect their children from others' comparisons that have the most impact on their kids.

WHAT IS SIBLING RIVALRY?

All kids at one point in their lives will compete with their brothers or sisters, whether it's to jockey for a better position in the family's pecking order, to get additional attention from Mom or Dad, or simply to claim ownership of something. Even the best-behaved kids in the world will occasionally compete with their siblings for bragging rights as the champion Monopoly player. It's a normal part of growing up in any family. Rivalry can be more frequent, however, when siblings are close in age than when they're spaced several years apart. And you can't get any closer in age to a sibling than when you're a multiple. So if you have a set or twins, triplets, or quads, does that mean they're destined to be rivalrous? Of course not. In fact some twins, especially identical twins, compete very little and instead prefer to cooperate with each other.

Making Comparisons—the Beginning of Sibling Rivalry

All families make comparisons among their children. But while these comparisons can be emotionally detrimental to singletons and multiples when done on a continual basis, they tend to be much more magnified in families with multiples. Parents expect their single-born children to excel in different areas since they usually have vastly different interests and aptitudes, thereby lessening comparisons made between them. When an older son shines as a top high school quarterback, for instance, while his younger brother has absolutely no interest in sports but prefers music, each is usually allowed his individual preferences with little or no comparisons made between the two. Yet in families with multiples, friends often notice the discrepancy between the pair and insist on asking, "Why isn't Johnny playing football, too?" or "Funny how Johnny isn't an accomplished football player like his twin brother." Since the two boys are exactly the same age, living under one roof, measuring one against the other is simply too tempting for many.

The problem with these comparisons is that whenever we differentiate between two things, there is often clearly a winner and a loser. "I like chocolate better than vanilla," and "I love the snow in winter, but I hate the heat in summer." With children it's no different. Even a simple comparison of Johnny's preference for music over football can be misconstrued as a preference for one child to the other. And if comparisons are made freely in a family, all at one child's expense, he often will inevitably begin to see himself as "less than."

The Difference Between Favorable and Unfavorable Comparisons. Most parents try to discourage outsiders from comparing their twins, but many may find it difficult not to do it themselves. This is not necessarily a bad thing in and of itself; it's when parents contrast their children openly and frequently for all to hear that this habit can be troubling. Often parents compare with the best intentions, too, such as congratulating one child for a job well done. But a favorable comparison such as "Great job on your spelling test! You're a much better speller than your brother" can actually have an unsettling effect on your good student. Although you meant well and only wanted to boost the child's self-confidence, motivating him to continue with the good work, your twin realizes that in order to keep on winning your approval he now needs to remain a better speller than his brother. His success was at his cotwin's expense and will have to remain that way. This can leave many children feeling anxious. And don't think his cotwin didn't notice your slight either. He may not verbalize his hurt feelings, but undoubtedly they'll have a negative impact.

On the other hand, some parents use unfavorable comparison as a way of forcing one child to change. Out of mere frustration you blurt out, "Your room is a pigsty. Why can't you pick up after yourself like your brother?" But the messy child rarely changes her ways, and now she just sees herself as lacking compared to her cotwin's standards. Worse, she thinks *you* think less of her.

Both of these comparisons—favorable and unfavorable— can have an adverse effect on the intratwin relationship by planting the seeds for a rivalry. A better tactic is to keep your observations, whether positive or negative, focused solely on the child in question, without mentioning the name of his cotwin—ever.

Comparing Discordant Twins. Unlike identical twins that share the same genetic makeup, fraternal twins share approximately 50 percent of their DNA. Therefore, genetically they are no more alike than any other two siblings born in different years. And just like single-born children, DZ twins often develop at different rates cognitively, socially, and physically. Yet society—family, friends, teachers, and sometimes strangers—continues to compare them against each other rather than against their peer group. When one twin walks at ten months, for instance, while the other doesn't take his first step until twelve months, the former is considered the "advanced" twin, even though both children learned to walk within the normal range.

The problem can persist in the school years when twin siblings are compared scholastically against one another. (Identical twins are hardly immune to scholastic comparisons either. Since MZ twins are often parallel physically, emotionally, and cognitively, even slight differences in school performance are noticed.) Once again, if one twin doesn't reach a benchmark as quickly as her cotwin, she could be unfairly labeled as

---

From One Parent to Another

"One of our twins (DZOS) tends to be academically competitive and always wants to know how they did compared to their twin. I worry that this particular twin's self-esteem might be somewhat wrapped up in always wanting or needing to outperform their sibling, and that their twin might worry a bit if they always wind up a close second. The kids compare themselves, too. This started when they were about four or five, 'Who walked first? Who talked first?' I would respond, 'Erica walked first, and Chris talked first.' It's inevitable that they'll compare themselves to one another, and I believe that even if you tell them not to verbalize it, they will be doing it internally. The kids each have a lot of strengths, and it's easy to remind them that one of them is always going to be either 'first at' or 'better at' something. We do not, however, allow boasting."

"struggling." Both can be intelligent, but if one does even slightly better academically, he's considered the "gifted" one. These labels are often unfair, as a difference between the twins does not necessarily signify a difference when compared to the population as a whole. The problem for both twin types can be compounded when the "struggling" twin is partnered up in class with her "gifted" twin under the pretext of helping her. The teacher may mean well by pairing these two up, but both can suffer here—the "struggling" twin continues to believe she's not as intelligent as her twin (why else, she thinks, would her teacher have paired her with the cotwin) and may never realize her full potential, while the "gifted" twin is held back and is given the awesome task of tutoring his cotwin. In this instance, separate classrooms would allow both children to learn at their own pace and to be rewarded for their own achievements without being compared to their sibling.

For the Love of a Label. We've all done it before: "This is the musical one," or "He's our little math genius." Labeling children is understandable. Most of the time we don't even know that we're doing it. It just seems like a practical way of identifying each person, anointing him with a special quality. It's harmless, too, right? After all who wouldn't want to be known as musically talented or a math whiz? Even our unsavory labeling is often viewed as funny: "He's our troublemaker," or "He was born a devil." Yet just like a label stubbornly glued on a jar, these seemingly innocent imprints stick. Even when they've long been outgrown, childhood labels are long lasting.

As kids grow up, labels are suddenly no longer cute but rather restrictive to their development. The math whiz has become tired of the subject and would prefer to write poetry, but something inside tells him, no, math is his thing, not poetry. When Mom or Dad give notice and attention to the "messy twin," even in a negative way, the child comes to see being messy as his role; the behavior is reinforced and ultimately continues. Most important, however, is how twins often reluctantly live up to their labels within the twinship as a way of being seen as individuals. When it comes to behaving, twins often go in opposite directions—if one is labeled "the good twin," the other twin, realizing the role is already taken, finds other, more negative ways of receiving parental attention. Thus he becomes "the bad twin." When one cotwin is constantly congratulated for her musical abilities and referred to as "our little Mozart," her cotwin may choose to ignore music altogether even if she'd like to study it and instead concentrate on sports just to be seen as different.

From One Parent to Another

"I think that people naturally want to label twins, not because they are trying to make a comparison, but as a way to distinguish them, to identify them, to help themselves remember who is who. Todd (DZSSm) recently confided that when he constantly heard himself described by friends and classmates as 'the smart one,' while Dan was 'the outgoing one,' that he felt more self-conscious about his social skills. As a result, he feels he became even less outgoing because he worried that he did not have what it takes. Perhaps Dan (DZSSm) was less inclined to put a lot of effort into academics in high school because he felt he would never be 'the smart one.'"

When Multiples Turn the Comparisons to Each Other

Not long ago, I met an adult MZ twin who related an interesting and even funny tale about his relationship with his cotwin. Both ran track and field and competed in a race together—one hundred meter sprint—along with four other competitors. The starting pistol rang out, but both boys quickly fell behind and finished fifth and sixth. Still, one twin was jubilant as he crossed the finish line. "I've won! I've won!" he yelled. He hadn't won the race—he finished fifth—he'd just beaten his twin. And to this doppelgänger that was more important.

As children get older, for some nearly everything becomes a competition. And when you have two children born on the same day sharing the same house, developing closely both cognitively and physically while everyone from their family to their classmates reminds them of their differences, it seems everything becomes a contest between the two—from who's taller to who got the higher test score.

The good news is that even through all of the fighting and bickering between twin pairs, there is a silver lining—a certain amount of sibling struggle is perfectly normal and actually helpful. Remember, all kids quarrel with each other. It's just that in families with multiples there seems to be a bit more behind the fighting than meets the eye. Twin conflict, especially during the preteen and teenage years, is just their way of struggling to find out who they are separate from their cotwin. In other words, they're growing up struggling to be seen as individuals.

Competition and Twin Type. Comparisons and subsequent competition between twins may be more obvious in families with multiples, but fortunately, research data suggests that twins are no more competitive than single-born children. The difference lies in the nature of the competition. Different-age children within the same family compete on different developmental levels, whereas multiples compete with each other at the same level and often in the same arenas. With that said, however, there does seem to be some clear competitive differences among twin types. For instance, identical twins appear to be the least rivalrous of all the twin subgroups (although some parents told me their MZ twins can often go at it). MZ and DZ twins use birth order as a power-wielding tool, "I was born first, so therefore I should get to go first!" It's interesting to note that with

> ### From One Parent to Another
>
> "When they were younger, they were much fiercer rivals. I can remember discussions about who got a better grade on a test, who had a better teacher, and who got better Valentines. I used to joke that I only had to teach one child how to do anything and the other would learn just to keep up. I know that Suzanne (MZf) learned to ride a bike because she wasn't going to let Elise (MZf) get too far ahead of her. They've improved a lot on that score with some of it having to do with being in completely different classes in junior high."

opposite-sex twins, birth order usually isn't a problem, but rather the focus is on their sex. "I'm the boy, so I should be able to pick the TV show."

Several research studies have looked into the relationship between cooperation and genetic relatedness—that is, are twins who are more similar in DNA more cooperative with each other? One recent study done by Nancy Segal at California State University in Fullerton, California, used the Prisoner's Dilemma game where cooperation between two twin players is beneficial to both but exploitation of one's partner offers a chance for higher personal gain to the exploiter. The results confirm what past research has shown—identical twins as a subgroup are more cooperative with each other than

From One Parent to Another

"It's hard not to compare Karsen and Kaden (MZm), especially since they are so identical, but I definitely try to avoid it. They're playing sports now, which is fueling the competition between them, and it pushes them each to try harder. They don't get mad at each other if one is doing something better— the other one just pushes himself more to catch up. I don't want them to feel like they have to always beat each other, though, so we try to encourage skills more than winning, but it's difficult."

same-sex, nonidentical twins. This is not to say that cooperation is a behavior inherent to identical twins, since when each was paired with a non–genetically related partner they were not more cooperative. In fact, they were more competitive.

So why is it that MZ twins cooperate more with each other than the other twin subgroups? Psychologists have varying opinions. The most plausible answer, however, lies within their genes —identical twins who share 100 percent of their DNA have a greater social closeness and have many more similar behavioral and physical characteristics than DZ twins. Since their identity is so tightly wound up in each other, identical twins show greater control when it comes to self-interest than other twin types. Feelings of jealousy and rivalry for the identical twin may be just too difficult to tolerate, and therefore, to circumvent the problem, MZ twins will choose to cooperate rather than compete with each other.

The Downside to Rivalry. Although a little competition between twins can be beneficial, sometimes it can lead to dangerous behavior, especially when the focus of the rivalry is unhealthy, such as weight loss. Twin or triplet girls may engage in an unspoken competition about who can become thinner. Parents need to be keenly aware if a daughter whose weight is within the normal range for her height begins to lose pounds just to catch up to her sister. Family members can aggravate the situation, too. For instance, if Mom obsessively focuses on her own body image, constantly struggling to achieve the perfect Hollywood figure, she could unwittingly fuel the fire to shed pounds. Instead parents should model healthy attitudes toward weight by being accepting of their own bodies and those they see in public as well as their daughters'. Furthermore, parents should never allow other members of the family to tease their siblings (or anyone, really) about body weight and image.

Still, you can't control what others say about your children. One mom told me that her relatives often compared her teenage MZ daughters' weight right in front of them. Realizing that this could be taken to heart,

> ### From One Parent to Another
>
> "I think people think it's funny or interesting to ask, 'Are you the good twin or the bad twin?' Or 'Which one is smarter or more athletic?' About a year ago at a family gathering I finally lost it and told an aunt that James and Rick (MZm) were two different people and that neither of them was worse than the other. I said she needed to stop labeling them and told her how much it had hurt my one son. No matter who it is, you need to step in and stop it right away. People don't realize how much children take to heart what adults say and how deeply words can cut. Pull the person to the side and help her realize what she just said."

this mom took action by diverting the conversation until the girls left the room and then making it clear to those engaging in the comparisons that it was not allowed. "There was nothing delicate that we could do," she said. "We were just in their faces about that one. I had to be to protect my daughters."

For some multiples, especially MZ twins who innately have similar likes and talents, a rivalry can be uncomfortable to their union. Let's use two track stars as an example—both are very good, but one always comes in first while the other second. It causes pain for both—the winner can't fully enjoy his accomplishments since he always sees the disappointment of his losing brother. Ultimately, some completely give up the sport in which they both excelled for fear of harming their relationship. A solution to this dilemma, however, can be as simple as choosing different areas within track and field in which to shine—"Twin A" can concentrate on sprinting, while "Twin B" can compete in long-distance running. This way the two can encourage each other free from guilt. Many multiples instinctively choose this healthy path rather than giving up a sport they love altogether; others may need gentle direction from their parents.

When Should Parents Step In? Parents need to be keenly aware when competition between their twins begins to get out of hand. The first sign is when one suddenly opts out of the same sport as his cotwin where he once found great pleasure. Remind your child to concentrate on his personal best rather than comparing himself to his twin. Besides, junior high and high school sports shouldn't be all about winning; shouldn't they be just for fun? Consider having a private chat with his cotwin, too, asking if he could offer positive encouragement to his struggling twin. Just knowing his cotwin is on his side is often enough to turn them into cooperating teammates, but if the struggling twin continues to show signs of frustration even after your and his cotwin's pep talks and it's having a negative impact on his relationship with his twin, consider allowing the child to quietly leave. No one wants to teach children, especially multiples, to become "quitters," but if your twin continues to show signs that he or she is uncomfortable in the shadow of his cotwin, maybe it's time to try something different and unique to just that child.

And although rare, step in when the verbal attacks turn vicious or when someone's in physical danger. But avoid becoming your twins' constant mediator, always judging who's wrong and who's right. You need to be impartial and to teach them both to work out their differences in constructive ways.

What Parents Can Do

Although your identical twins may not tolerate competing against one another, some MZ twins by the nature of their environment, surroundings, and even upbringing may succumb. Other twin types may feel the need to compete with one another as well. Just remember: whenever you gauge one child through the actions of another, you can't help but draw a comparison. To combat rivalry and instead encourage cooperative behavior between your multiples, fight the urge to compare them by following these tricks.

- Don't assume that your twins enjoy the public attention from others curious about their relationship—many twins are very uncomfortable when strangers and family members compare them. Practice several scripts with your twins for awkward situations when outsiders ask probing questions. For instance, when someone inquires, "Who's older?" or "Who's smarter?" help your twins come up with a witty response (and even role-play their answers) that will succinctly yet politely let the person know that the question is an old one. ("Who's smarter?" "Only after we leave our brains to science will we know for sure.") If family members and friends continue to compare your multiples, speak with them in private, politely explaining why you'd like them to stop the practice.
- Fight the urge yourself to compare them, at least out loud. Keep reprimands and issues of discipline focused on the child in question, and never bring in her cotwin as a comparison. Instead of saying, "You're always late. I expect you

to be home on time like your sister," try, "You need to make every effort to be home on time for dinner. If you find that you simply can't, please call." In addition, keep compliments to the individual, not the pair. For instance, replace "What a great job you did on your book report. You got a higher grade than even your brother" with "Congratulations! You worked hard on that book report, and it shows."

- Don't overreact to sibling disputes since it can sometimes fuel their rivalry. Don't step in and try to solve their problems, but don't turn a deaf ear either—you'll only explode when their quarreling escalates. Instead, when you sense a fight brewing, act from the sidelines by reminding each child of the right way to disagree—listening to each other, negotiating, and coming to a mutual compromise.

- Encourage all family members to not only root for their siblings when they reach an accomplishment but to also offer solace when they fall short. Notice when they act compassionately toward each other and praise them for it.

- When it comes to school, never allow teachers to compare the grades of one twin to those of the other. Insist on knowing how each individual compares to the class as a whole. When setting up appointments to discuss your children's progress in school, always set up two different appointments. It requires more time but sends an important message of how you'd like your children to be treated.

- Find that balance between praising one without diminishing the other. It's fine to congratulate one child in front of his cotwin since the cotwin needs to understand that it's normal and OK to feel both jealousy and pride at the same time. In addition, however, offer private congratulations to the achiever. It shows the successful twin that you have indeed noticed his accomplishments but not at the expense of his cotwin. Furthermore, offer the twin who missed out on the award a chance to vent his frustrations and jealousy. Offer encouragement and remind him of his past achievements. All of this should be done without taking on his anger and pain—take on the role of sympathetic listener instead.

- Downplay their birth order. Don't cast twins into the role of "older" and "younger" since the "older" will lord it over the "younger," setting off a rivalry in the process as the "older" tries to uphold his rank and the "younger" works fiercely to undo it. This is especially important when twins are the only children in the family and the temptation to designate older and younger roles is stronger. Instead give each child equal opportunity to be the responsible one, the one who gets to go first. For instance, let them take turns taking the note to the teacher, carrying the house key, using the computer first, signing the family Christmas card, and so on.

- If twins get caught up in the comparison game themselves ("Hey, I got a higher grade than you on last week's spelling test!"), butt out and let them get bored with the discussion themselves. By calling attention to it, even to tell them to stop, puts too much emphasis on it and encourages them to do it more. A better tactic is to divert the conversation, "Hey, who wants to rent a movie?"

From One Parent to Another

"I made a big mistake. I let Cortney (DZSSf) be reliant for both of them. If they had to take money to school or anything important, I gave it to Cortney because I knew she wouldn't lose it. Then I thought about it and realized I wasn't making Amber responsible for anything—I was making Cortney responsible for it all. I was cheating them both. To this day, Amber's not really responsible."

- Examine your personal views of competition—if your family has the "gotta get ahead" and "win at all costs" attitude, then your multiples may internalize those sentiments as well. Instead, downplay competition and promote the benefits of teamwork, cooperation, and pulling together as a family. Praise them when they act kindly toward each other. Help them see and appreciate the strengths in each other and to show that appreciation to each other often.

- If your twins are uncomfortable with the constant comparisons made at school, consider placing them in separate classrooms. If the comparisons continue to escalate, dampening your twins' relationship, you may want to think about separate schools if your twins are open to the idea. Physical space between the pair may be just what they crave in order to pursue their own interests at their own pace. Several families I interviewed for this book enrolled their middle and high school multiples in separate institutions with positive results.

After-School Activities

For many twins, participating in the same after-school activities such as team sports and social clubs never presents a problem (all three of my boys have successfully been in the same karate class for nearly two years). MZ twins are often drawn to the exact same clubs and teams because of their identical genetic makeup. Some multiples make great teammates, too, helping each other perfect their form. Others relish going against a matched opponent any time of the day. For parents, it sometimes becomes a matter of practicality, too—it's infinitely easier to have all multiples together in one spot concentrating on one sport at the same time. (No one enjoys being a taxicab driver every afternoon.)

After-School Activities *(continued)*

Yet for those who are forced into the same sports or activities simply for the sake of convenience, it may not work out well. What happens if they differ in ability and one cotwin can't compete at the same level as his brother? Or what if another cotwin simply doesn't have the same interests as her sister? Parents should take their signals from their kids and be sensitive to their interests and skill level.

- While no parent wants to encourage a child to become a quitter, some multiples have unspoken reasons for wanting to stop playing a particular sport or being a member of a specific social club. Be sensitive to the reasons why your child doesn't want too participate—does she feel overshadowed by her cotwin even though it's something she loves, too? Perhaps attending different classes at different times or on different days is the answer. Or is she continuing in a sport that she has little interest or talent in simply because she doesn't want to miss out on parental approval for her efforts?
- Don't focus solely on the "superstar" player and his accomplishments, dismissing the supporting player of your family. Doing so will only increase competition between the pair. Instead praise effort, cooperation, and solidarity. Remind your kids that competing in sports is just plain fun—learning a new skill tops the list; winning should be secondary.
- Be open to experimentation—one twin may want to try something unique and different from her cotwin, a sport or an activity where she can shine alone. Allow her the option to try.

THE POSITIVE SIDE TO TWIN COMPETITIVENESS

Last summer at my local pool, one twin decided he wanted to learn how to dive. After a few prompts from me, he was nearly a pro, quickly graduating from the side of the pool to the diving

---

From One Parent to Another

"Sometimes Victoria and Kate (MZf) pick a swim stroke to be best at—Victoria the butterfly or free, Kate the backstroke or free. They've competed in head-to-head races and in relays and decided to win whenever they could, even if it meant touching out the other at the wall. I'm proud at how healthy their competition has been so far. I hope this competition stays healthy, especially through the middle and high school years. It's not easy to be a girl that looks just like another girl."

---

board. I sat at the sidelines cheering him on as any proud mom would do. Within the hour, however, his cotwin got wind of what was going on. Whether he wanted that positive approval from me, couldn't bear his brother mastering a skill that he hadn't, or it just looked like a lot of fun, it didn't take long before he, too, was up on that diving board shouting, "Hey, Mom, watch me!" before plunging into the water headfirst.

Who says that all sibling rivalry is bad? It can run the spectrum, however, from one extreme to the other—from that of constant sibling tension and emotional pain to that of playful banter where both parties find verbal sparring not only interesting but the building blocks to a strong, mature relationship. For most kids, sibling rivalry and cooperation swing both ways from the occasional, "I want to kill you!" to "You're my best friend" and just about everything else in between.

But what are the advantages to competing with one's cotwin? Plenty, the experts say. Many believe it helps develop personality and ego. In other words, kids who compete with each other have a stronger sense of autonomy and higher individuation, which, as you have read in past chapters, is essential for every child, yet is sometimes harder for multiples to develop. Competition often acts as a stimulus to achieve to a greater degree, too. If a cotwin sees his brother trying hard and

receiving accolades for his success, he may push himself a bit
more, too. But for the most part,
the sibling bond, even when rife
with competitiveness, teaches
children coping strategies for the
future and how to socialize in
the world at large.

The Great Debaters

Although twins are often wonderful companions, they also
make even better sparring partners. Yet is this so bad? It may be
hard for parents to listen to their
kids fighting, but many of these
word wars can actually help mul-

> **From One Parent to Another**
>
> "They have always helped each
> other in school, but now they seem
> to be more competitive toward
> each other. Yet it's helped because
> if one gets a lower grade it spurs
> him on to do better. What's inter-
> esting, though, is that if one gets a
> lower grade they usually commiser-
> ate with each other. So if Allan
> (MZm) gets an A in reading and
> Alexander (MZm) gets a B, Alexan-
> der is compelled to do better next
> time, but Allan lets him know that
> it's OK if he doesn't."

tiples develop a finesse for negotiation. Through making their
point of view known they learn to manage and resolve conflicts, or at the very least encourage great debates, as each tries
to convincingly get his point across to his cotwin. In short,
they learn how to work out problems on their own (if parents
can stay out of their way and let them, that is). These are all
social skills that children learn early and once mastered can be
used successfully as adults when dealing with future peers, partners, and even business associates.

Academic Decathlon

In our elementary school we have an independent reading program where kids read whatever books they'd like at their own
pace and then take comprehension tests on the ones they've

From One Parent to Another

"Guinevere and Meredith (MZf) are almost constantly in competition. For instance, we gave Meredith a book for Christmas that she was very excited about and began telling the story to Guinevere. Guinevere became interested but couldn't wait for Meredith to finish reading the book, so Guin checked it out from the school library. The competition is, for the most part, friendly—there's no taunting or other mean-spirited comparison. I think this has led them to be more accomplished and more outgoing since they get double exposure to a lot of things."

completed. They score points and win medallions based on their individual achievement. When one of my sons heard that his brother recently moved up a notch into the next level, it spurred him to do more independent reading to try to catch up. What started as a necessity to him turned into a hobby—he now reads as voraciously as his brother. Now, is that so bad?

Many twins compete academically with their cotwins, whether consciously or unconsciously. If both twins are on the same developmental level, this will often work to their advantage as each strives to do even better.

From One Parent to Another

"Interestingly, in their freshman year, Todd and Dan (DZSSm) refused to play together as a doubles tennis team because this seemed to be too 'twinny' to them. Instead, they were each part of a doubles team, only with different partners. They also played as singles one year, rather than pair up. However, by their senior year, they realized that no one would think they were being 'twinny' by playing together, and they also recognized they could be very successful if they joined forces!"

AND THEY ALL LIVED
HAPPILY EVER AFTER

Comparing and contrasting your multiples is probably inevitable (as you already know), but it doesn't have to be harmful to their relationship. Loving, cooperative relationships between all family members are possible if you try to keep unnecessary or potentially harmful comparisons and comments to yourself. Remind yourself and your children that everyone will excel and even struggle at different things and at different times in their lives. Yet when it comes to outsiders, always step in before their comparisons make their way to your multiples. Remember, you're your children's strongest advocate.

6

Rethinking Fairness
and Fighting Favoritism

Remember those first few birthday, Christmas, and Hanukkah presents you gave your multiples? If you're like most parents with twins, you probably gave your kids exactly the same gift (two matching tricycles, for instance), complementary toys (one that would work well with the other such as two sets of the same Lego theme or two Barbies dressed in different outfits), or the same gift in different colors (red and blue Game Boys, for instance). We all did it! First of all, it prevented intratwin squabbles just as long as you got the color right. Even though we know that we needn't and shouldn't treat twins the same, it just seemed easier sometimes, less of a headache. Besides, something inside us told us that if we didn't give matching gifts somehow we were favoring one twin over the other.

Surely by now your twins are showing preferences for different toys, books, and gadgets that you oblige every year, but you're probably still finding ways to ensure that everything is even-steven. Maybe now you calculate the number of gifts and their cost to make sure they're about the same. Yet if your son

From One Parent to Another

"I automatically assume that I'm going to have to think of some compensation for one (MZm) if the other gets something. I understand in theory that it's really important for them to know that there are times when one of them will get something and the other won't, and that's the way life is. The world provides those opportunities—I find it hard to provide them myself. When it happens out there in the world, I don't go to extra lengths to fix it. I do try to acknowledge the sadness about it though."

needs a new pair of gym shoes, do you feel compelled to buy the other a pair as well? If one needs some private time with you to share her bad day at school, do you call the other in afterward to spend an equal amount of alone time? And what if you have triplets or quads? Making sure things are perfectly even can sure add up.

Why do you do it? Maybe you bend over backward to make things fair because you think you should love them equally. Or maybe, just maybe, you try to treat each multiple the same as a way of compensating for guilty feelings of liking or enjoying the company of one child more than the other. Favoritism, although it exists in nearly all families to a certain degree (and isn't more common in a family with multiples), does seem to be more glaring, more conspicuous when it happens in a family with twins or triplets. It's an emotion that's not only difficult to talk about but even harder to admit to feeling.

I JUST WANT TO BE FAIR

What's your definition of fair? The dictionary says, "Free from bias, dishonesty, or injustice." It doesn't say, "To treat everyone in a manner that is exactly the same." Yet as a loving parent, you don't want to show any hint of partiality. After all, you want all your children, especially your multiples, to know that they are loved equally. But is it possible to love equally? Do you need to love equally?

In your day-to-day dealings with your family, are you always monitoring yourself for fairness toward all of your children? You're not alone if you do. I remember once when my boys were toddlers we ventured to the supermarket for our weekly groceries. At the checkout counter, each boy received a balloon from the cashier, but by the time we reached the car, one son had let his go. Tears and screams of frustration bellowed from the twin who had lost his, his hand reaching out toward his brother's bright red balloon. Pressed for time, I couldn't return to get another one, so my first thought was to take away the other child's balloon so that I'd even out the situation. Insane, right? Yet I just wanted everything to be fair, even if it meant both of them crying. Fortunately, I resisted the urge and offered lots of hugs to my crying son instead.

> ### From One Parent to Another
>
> "We always try to be fair—it just happens that way. As a mother I am very aware of this issue. Now that they are older, they want different things, but it is still hard for me to get it for one and not the other. This last Christmas, Ryan (zygosity unknown) made a list of things he would like to have; Christopher didn't make a list but only asked for a new watch. I ended up getting Christopher most of the same type things that Ryan asked for, and I bought them both a new watch. I tried not to do it, but I couldn't help myself. I hate the idea of one thinking he received less than his brother. At the same time, we know that the world is not fair and struggle to help them understand that everything will not always be equal for them."

All the parents I interviewed for this book second-guessed themselves when it came to showing love and affection and doling out treats to their multiples. Some even confided that they went to extra lengths to even the playing field. One mom told me that when one child was accepted into the gifted program in school and the other wasn't, she secretly declined the offer in fear that having only one enroll would set up a rivalry between her sons. Another mom had a similar story—there were only a certain number of spots for the school science fair, and the lucky participants were to be chosen by lottery. Nervous that only one of her sons would be chosen, she convinced the teachers to put both boys' names on one sheet of paper.

I'm sure you have stories to tell, too. Perhaps you've felt guilty when you've had a playful romp on the living room floor with one twin. The other, having seen all the fun, demanded equal time but you needed to go and start cooking dinner or get ready for work. Guilt took over as you walked away and the cotwin whined, "It's not fair!" Or perhaps you've called one child over to enjoy a song or book you knew she'd appreciate, yet in the back of your head you felt guilty for not including the other.

Parents of multiples always seem to measure their actions, making certain all siblings receive equal amounts of love, attention, and yes, even dessert. It's as if there's an internal scale inside every mom weighing her every move and notating what she gives to each twin.

Why We Do It and Why We Need to Stop

Most school-age twins demand that parents treat them fairly, and to them that often means the same. "If she got a new pair of leather boots, then I want a pair, too!" Parents, not wanting to show preferential treatment, try to offer it, and many times give each twin exactly what the other has whether or not she needs it. If your daughter insists on staying up until ten o'clock just like her cotwin, but she had a sleepover the night before and is exhausted, you're likely to give in, even if it's not best for her.

Yet parenting experts agree: it's actually unfair to try to treat each multiple exactly the same. First, no matter how much they look alike, they're different and unique people with different needs. When you treat all multiples exactly the same, you inadvertently deny their individuality. It's never really possible to treat all your children exactly the same way, and you shouldn't try. Twins make a clever pair, and if they see that you doubt your parenting skills and give in to their demands ("He got new jeans, so I should get a pair, too!"), they will soon realize that their joint pressure yields a lot of power in your household. One twin researcher pointed out that if opposite-sex twins are constantly treated similarly, always offered the same in the way of attention and possessions, parents may in fact be treating them as a unisex pair, depriving them of their inherent sexuality. Whether or not you view that statement as a stretch, the principal idea rings true—you shouldn't automate your responses to your twins. All children should be treated uniquely based on need. And that's the true meaning of fairness.

Moreover, you're not doing your multiples any favor by sheltering them from unfairness; by the time they grow up and are out of the house, they'll quickly realize that the world is in fact an unfair place. As they advance through school, one or the other is bound to receive an award for a particular

---

From One Parent to Another

"We instilled in the girls pretty early that we don't buy stuff for no reason in our house. Sheila (DZSSf) would always notice 'unfairness' more and speak about it, while Ginny was quiet about it. And then one day you'd find Ginny in her room crying about it. If you'd say, 'what's wrong?' she'd come up with all this stuff that was bothering her, and one would be, 'You bought Sheila a pair of jeans, and you didn't buy one for me.' I'd hug her and kiss her and tell her I love her and then say, 'You don't need a pair of jeans.'"

achievement, leaving the other to lament, "It's not fair! I should have gotten one, too!" What will you do? Insist the one who didn't get an award get one too? Or worse, don't let the achiever receive his accolades? Instead, as a parent your responsibility is to gently point out the way of the world and let the one who didn't receive the award air his feelings of futility.

It's perfectly normal for one twin to feel both jealous and happy when his cotwin achieves something he didn't, but it's important for the child on the losing end to congratulate his cotwin. It's part of being a member of the family. Feeling jealous and happy at the same time may seem contradictory, but it's perfectly normal and should be validated. Remind the twin on the losing end that there will always be differences between the two in nearly every aspect of their lives—socially, academically, physically. Help him to see that this one rejection isn't forever—he'll have plenty of opportunities to shine on his own. Rather than protecting children from inevitable disappointments, parents, family members, and even teachers need to help their multiples understand and accept rejection as a part of life.

What Parents Can Do

Every parent wants to show her children that she loves them wholly and equally. Yet that doesn't mean you have to literally give each child equal amounts of everything. Here are a few other ideas to fight the fairness fever.

- Think unique. You needn't love your children equally but rather uniquely. Each child has something special to offer and, consequently, has individual talents and personality quirks. Focus on loving those attributes that make each of your children exceptional.
- Never downplay, ignore, or in some way diminish one twin's accomplishment for the sake of sparing the other

twin's feelings. Parents shouldn't downplay ("Don't get so upset that your brother won. It was just the school science fair, not a national one") or even deny one twin's achievement, such as winning a scholarship, merely because his cotwin did not. In addition, parents need to think twice before offering an incentive (like a new car) to both twins to reach some sort of goal, be it academic, athletic, or even social. What happens when only one twin reaches that goal? What message is it sending to the twin who simply can't meet the challenge?

- Teach your children how to be good sports—encourage your multiples to sincerely congratulate each other regardless of negative feelings. Remind each child that it's not a competition between just the two of them. Praise them when they compliment each other.

- Because of their shared environment and development, multiples need a bit of extra help in dealing with the negative feelings of jealousy and anger that occur when one receives or earns something that the other does not. Parents, teachers, and even coaches all need to be aware of the complexities of the multiple relationship. They shouldn't

---

From One Parent to Another

"I would always give Ande and A.J. (DZOS) the same everything—the same amount of food, the same number of shirts, shorts, shoes. If one wanted a toy I had to get one for the other one. Yet I'm finding that it is more my problem than theirs. They really don't seem to care now that they're spending some of their own money. I struggled with it because I didn't want them to think I was favoring one more because one needed something. I'm getting better now that I am realizing that they have different wants and needs."

make extra efforts to even out the situation but rather help the disappointed twin deal with the feelings of failure.

UNDERSTANDING FAVORITISM

Favoritism—preferring the company of one child to all the others—happens to some degree in nearly all families. In healthy families, though, one child is not the perennial favorite. Each child is favored for different characteristics or at different times in life. Furthermore, well-functioning parents recognize their preferences and make conscious attempts at keeping all the relationships balanced.

Interestingly, studies indicate that larger families may have a better hold on favoritism than smaller families, since parents with a lot of kids have to spread their love around to many. Their offspring, in turn, often feel like a team working together toward a common goal. In addition, kids from large families often buddy up with another sibling, a playmate and constant companion, thereby compensating for days when Mom or Dad may need to devote extra time and attention to one particular child in the family.

Sometimes in families with single-born children, the issue of favoritism is not nearly as perceptible since parents can easily qualify their preferences: "She's my little girl. Even her older brothers adore her," or "He's the

---

From One Parent to Another

"I have felt favoritism, but I think it has to do with having more in common with the favored one. I would feel guilty that I wasn't spending enough time with the other twin (DZSSf), and I would try to put more effort into that relationship. Also with the younger set of twins (DZSSf), one is more sensitive than the other and I tend to draw nearer to her. But at the same time, I recognize that the other twin may be acting up more just to get my attention. So I try to see to her needs, too."

oldest and the most dependable of all his siblings." Yet in families with twins, especially where the twins are the only children the parents have, a preference for one over the other can be glaring and conspicuous, at least to the parent who feels it. While the attachment may not be out of the ordinary, the guilt associated with preferring one to the other can be harmful to a family. If not dealt with in a healthy manner, favoritism can become insidious and long lasting.

How Does It Begin?

Favoritism has a way of creeping into families. Many different explanations exist for its development, especially for families with multiples, whose mother's experience is very different from those families with single-born children. For instance, a mom having just given birth to twins may find herself preferring the heavier baby even when the cotwin is healthy and of adequate weight. Some speculate that perhaps the smaller baby is the manifestation of the mother's prenatal anxieties. She had worried for months that her children would be born underweight, and now one is in fact smaller. Just what she had feared. On the other hand, some mothers prefer the "easier baby," one who fusses less, sleeps more soundly, or nurses voraciously. Often when multiples are very young, one parent seems to have a certain finesse with one baby more than the other—Dad can make little Johnny stop crying better than Mom. But what starts out as something practical ("Please take him, he's crying again") can turn into something more long lasting, well past the crying stage. There's even a third scenario: since dads nearly always have to step up to the plate and help with early responsibilities of diapering and feeding, each parent can inadvertently take charge of just one baby. An innocent practicality can sometimes turn into a lifelong preference—he's "Mom's baby" and she's "Dad's baby."

Another study found that many parents have a stronger preference for the twin who simply left the hospital first. In the study of 166 sets of twins, 35 pairs left the hospital at varying times, while the remaining 131 sets left the same day. Mothers were then asked about their feelings for each twin. The twins who left at the same time were both viewed favorably by their mothers, yet those multiples who left the hospital at different times were regarded differently—the child who left first was rated more positively than the cotwin left behind. The study further indicated that the longer the child was left in the newborn intensive care unit (NICU), the more negatively he was perceived by his mother. Even though he was perfectly healthy, in his mother's eyes he demanded more attention, was fussier and harder to manage than his cotwin.

It's understandable how this type of preference began. Mom is at home nurturing and bonding with her new baby while his cotwin is still in NICU. She develops a routine with the baby at home and may find it difficult to get to the hospital daily to see and hold her other child. Emotionally exhausted, she may be unconsciously reluctant to start the bonding process all over again when the cotwin is finally released. Although these reactions are normal, many mothers (and fathers) hide these negative feelings, and without support and reassurance, these preferences can continue on into their twins' adulthood. The implications of this study are very important as they point out the need to reevaluate if infant multiples should be discharged from the hospital at different times. Or, at the very least, hospitals may want to consider offering counseling to parents of multiples whose children are born prematurely and require a lengthy stay in the NICU.

Sometimes favoritism has to do with the roles children assume in the family. For instance, if one child has gone through a clumsy stage, constantly spilling her milk at the dinner table or

From One Parent to Another

"I tended to favor my son (DZOSm) because he was so much easier and a joy to be with. I took care of my daughter (DZOSf) and loved her, but it was always a struggle. I knew that I couldn't change her personality, so I had to work on myself to help her to grow. I tended to feel that my daughter never should have been a twin because she was so demanding of attention. If I patted her on the shoulder once and her brother twice, she noticed. If I served him first twice in a row, I heard about it. She always brought it to my attention. In fact, I swear that is how she learned to count."

accidentally dropping jars while helping to put away the groceries, when something goes wrong at home she may be automatically and unfairly accused. She may become resentful of the accusations and even begin to lie when she actually does break or spill something. The cotwin, in turn, may feel guilty for letting her twin take the fall and act especially good to counterbalance it. Soon a pattern emerges—the seemingly clumsy twin assumes her role, Mom or Dad reinforces it, the cotwin turns into the "good twin" to counterbalance the role of her sibling. And before you know it, a feeling of partiality grows.

Finally, sometimes twin type has to do with parental preference. When fraternal twins are dissimilar in character and appearance and they happen to be the only children in the family, sometimes each parent identifies with a different child. Mom may be drawn to the twin who looks more like her side of the family, while Dad may connect with the child whose temperament or interests are more in line with his. What starts out as an innocent sharing of similar interests or tastes can turn into a strong and perhaps unhealthy preference by each parent if left to grow.

The Consequences of Favoritism

Understand that parents always have a certain amount of favoritism or preference for one child over the others at one point or another, even in many families with just single-born children. Whether it's because of the child's temperament or interests—sports, music, art, science, fashion—parents understandably prefer to spend more time with that child. This is usually not a problem unless it's at the expense of the other siblings. However, too much identification with one child is never good as it can blur the line between parent and child, slowly fusing the two roles together. What would happen, for instance, if there were a divorce or death in the family that left the unfavored child emotionally exiled?

Favoritism also has an interesting effect on some twins. Because identical twins (MZ) have a strong connection with each other, they often avoid jealousy between them at all costs. Some instinctively make themselves as alike as possible to avoid jealousy. It's their thinking that if they're the same, they'll be given the same, loved the same, attended to in the same way. Or sometimes they each bond more closely with a different parent and then adopt that parent's role within the context of their relationship. This behavior is sometimes evident in younger twins, where one may mother the other or play the protector.

When Mom or Dad shows a bias for one child, the family dynamics become unbalanced. This imbalance can make the multiples feel unsafe, and many may not want to separate from each other, subsequently hampering their sense of individuality. The less-favored child may be afraid to spend time alone with the parent, knowing or sensing there's no connection, and will only venture out with Mom or Dad if his cotwin goes too, to act as his safety net. Sensing what's happening, the favored cotwin will often comply, wanting to protect his twin.

On rare occasions, if a twin feels that his cotwin is the preferred child, he'll emotionally bow out of the relationship in order to avoid a rivalry, or may form an unhealthy dependence on his cotwin as a way of getting closer to his parents. If he latches on to the favored cotwin, he thinks, he's sure to receive love and attention, too, if only by proxy. This toxic relationship can continue throughout their lives, with their twinship becoming a twisted oxymoron—a fierce rivalry but trusted companionship.

As a parent, it's an awful feeling when you prefer one child to the other. In response to those uncomfortable feelings, a parent may try to overcompensate by allowing the less-favored twin to get away with more at home and out in public, bending the rules more often than the family would normally allow. But instead of easing the guilt, this actually intensifies the negative feelings. It's a vicious circle—the unfavored child sees Mom's a pushover and continues behaving badly, reinforcing her original prejudice. On the other hand, if a parent remains steadfast with the ground rules, the child learns that negative behavior gets him nowhere. Eventually he'll toe the line, and most likely his positive actions will be looked upon more favorably as well.

Favoritism and Adolescence

While most empirical studies in the past have focused on the effects of favoritism on young multiples, what happens when these children grow up? Many recent studies are surfacing that address this question. One large, published study in particular looked at differing parental treatment—how a parent behaves toward one child relative to another child—and its effect on a child's attachment to his mother or father. Through confidential, standardized questionnaires, 174 teenage twins were asked to rate parental affection and control as well as their own social and personal self-esteem and anxiety to try to determine if there's a connection between perceived parental treatment and the twins' reported social adjustment. The results showed that in families where kids perceived different parental treatment, the unfavored child suffered from attachment insecurity, anxiety, and low self-esteem.

Furthermore, other studies indicate that perceived parental favoritism can be damaging to the adolescents' sibling relationships—both for the favored as well as the unfavored child. On the one hand, an unfavored child often feels hostile and jealous and is often more confrontational toward the cotwin who receives less parental discipline and more positive support. The favored child may feel enormous guilt for being preferred or may feel she has a lot at stake in maintaining her status as the likable child, resulting in higher levels of anxiety. Both unfavored and favored children were more destructive physically and verbally when it came to conflict resolution, too, and also viewed their parents more negatively than children in families where there was no favoritism. The result is often a relationship that is unbalanced and disruptive, a condition that may continue well into their adult lives.

In fact, another very recent study confirms that parental preference continues to have an effect on young adults' mental health. Researchers found that twenty-two to thirty-year-old twins who felt equally close to both their parents during childhood currently experienced less depression and nervousness than those who felt they were disfavored.

What Parents Can Do

If you feel drawn to one twin more than the other, realize that it's a normal emotion. Don't feel guilty! The trick, however, is not to show such feelings to the less-favored twin so that he feels unloved in any way. In addition, you should try to build a connection to that child. Accept that favoritism happens and that you're not a bad parent because of it. Realize, too, that favoritism for one child isn't fixed in stone—circumstances change as we all grow and mature. It's not only in the best interest of the parent-child bond to eliminate favoritism, but it will also have a positive impact on the intrasibling relationship. With that in mind, there are things that you can do now to balance the scales between the favored and unfavored child.

> **From One Parent to Another**
>
> "Although it's very difficult to admit it, I believed that one of my kids (MZm) loved me more than the other, which caused me to favor him. Now I think that the other one just had trouble expressing his feelings. Since he left for college, he is much better at expressing himself, and we both show our love more fully."

- Remember, you're the adult. You're the one who will need to change. Try to pinpoint what it is about the child that you find difficult and why and then work from there. Try not to have a knee-jerk reaction to her behavior—take a moment before responding. Simply acting more lovingly toward the less-favored child will help more positive feelings to follow. Consciously try to make yourself more available—both physically and emotionally—to the less-favored child.

- Spend more one-on-one time with the less-favored child either by going out alone together or by doing even simple projects together such as preparing the evening meal, reading a story together, or playing cards or a board game.

- Tap into the less-favored child's world, taking an interest in her life. Ask questions about her hobbies, her dreams for the future, and her favorite subjects in school, then try to find common ground. Show an interest by attending his baseball games or her gymnastics meets.

- No one is solely good or utterly bad. Focus on the qualities that you do enjoy or admire in the less-favored child and try to disregard or overlook the bad. Remember that balance is key to a well-functioning family.
- Keep issues of discipline one-on-one—never allow the favored child to act as a surrogate parent, offer an opinion, or to take sides against the less-favored child during a parent-child disagreement.
- Don't give in to your guilt by looking the other way when the less-favored twin does something wrong—discipline for this child should follow the house rules, too. Instead accept the preference as a fact of life (at least for now) and focus on loving and parenting properly.
- Allow your children to talk openly to help identify feelings of favoritism, or try not to be defensive if your spouse tries to point it out. Instead, remember that feelings of favoritism happen sometimes, and let yourself become aware of your actions toward the unfavored child.

From One Parent to Another

"My mother was the youngest of thirteen, and my grandmother had forty-four grandchildren, but when you were with her, she could make you feel like you were her favorite grandchild. And I've adopted the same attitude with my kids. Sometimes they (DZSSm) say, 'You love Rob [older, single-born son] the best.' And I say, 'No, I love him different. I love every one of you differently because there are unique things about each of you that make you so special.' I can't say that I love anyone more than the others, I just love them in different ways."

When Grandma Has a Favorite

You may not have a favorite, but perhaps a member of your family does. As hard as you might try to overlook it, Grandma or Grandpa continues to pay special attention to one of your multiples more than the others. Perhaps she gives more time and attention to the first grandson or granddaughter in the family with your multiples left sitting on the sidelines. In the case of racially mixed families, some grandparents are drawn more to the child (or children) who resembles their heritage or ethnicity. Or maybe you remarried several years ago, and your new in-laws are having a hard time viewing your twins as part of the family. It hurts you to watch as grandparents shower attention on their "pet" at the expense of your other children, but should you say something?

- Before you step in to confront the situation (and perhaps ruffle some feathers in the process), ask yourself a few questions: What is it exactly that makes you feel as though the grandparents are favoring one more than the other? Perhaps they're just expressing congratulations on an award or honor that only one multiple has attained? Make sure it's not just recognition for a job well done.
- If the favoritism is blatant and consistent, by all means step in. Find a private time when you can have a heart-to-heart conversation. Point out the ways in which you feel that the grandparent shows a bias, and offer ideas on what she can change (tune her into what the unfavored child is interested in, for instance).
- If the grandparent showers one twin with lots of presents and money but not the other, explain that in the future it's all or nothing—either she gives equally or not at all.
- If the preferential treatment continues even after you've expressed your feelings (she may deny ever doing it), you're perfectly within your rights to take the steps you need to protect your children, even if that means staying away. When the guilty party asks why you're not coming around any longer, be straightforward and tell her.

ALL'S FAIR THAT'S NOT FAIR

Although fairness and favoritism may seem at opposite ends of the spectrum, they have many elements in common. Well-functioning families are those that keep the love and attention flowing to all members of the clan and value each child for his or her own specialness, while channeling goodies like new shoes and blue jeans on a need-only basis. But keep your eyes and heart open to those times when you're giving too much time and merchandise to a child who doesn't need it while ignoring the one who does. It's only by recognizing favoritism within yourself that you can come to terms with it and ultimately put an end to it.

7

When They Reach Puberty: Multiples as Teenagers

Do you remember being a teenager? If you're like most adults, you'd probably love to regain that endless energy as well as the taut body, the feeling of camaraderie with same-sex friends, and the excitement of dating the opposite sex for the first time, but more than likely you wouldn't want to relive the angst and insecurity that also came along with that stage in life.

Adolescence is a time of great change physiologically, cognitively, and socially. Teenagers often welcome a shift in their identities, ridding themselves of outgrown childhood roles, and they look for affirmation from their peers and from themselves that they are indeed grown up. They dress differently, sometimes experiment with radical hairstyles (please, no purple hair), and some even take dangerous risks by dabbling with drugs and alcohol or even breaking the law. They test the boundaries (not to mention patience) of teachers, parents, siblings, and even their own friends. Yet is being an adolescent multiple any different than being an adolescent singleton? To a certain degree, the answer is yes. Is it more difficult? Probably not, the experts say. In fact, much of the research as well as anecdotal tales from the twins themselves confirm that the advantages outweigh the disadvantages.

THE ADVANTAGES OF BEING A TEENAGE MULTIPLE

No doubt that going through adolescence can be tough on all kids. Peer pressure, the need to be seen as different yet also a part of the crowd (never could figure that one out), raging hormones wreaking havoc on one's mind and body—it's a wonder anyone survives! Many parents I interviewed described their multiples' adolescence as a time of enormous love coupled with a bit of jealousy. Surprisingly, everyone survived just fine. While it's true that multiples experience additional obstacles (which we'll get into in a moment) as they navigate through the tempestuous preteen and teenage years, there are several distinct and important advantages to being a twin, triplet, or even quad. Many adult twins have even joked that if you're going to be a teenager, it's best to do it with a cotwin by your side.

For instance, as a teenager would you ever attend a popular party alone? No way. You wouldn't do it. You'd call every friend you had to see if one would go with you. With multiples, however, new and unfamiliar social situations aren't nearly as threatening since they're often in it together. The power and comfort of two or even three—whether hanging out at the coffeehouse or the Friday night football game—sounds better than that of a singleton braving these social waters alone any day. (Granted, many teenage twins prefer to hang out with their own individual friends rather than their cotwins, but others still count their cotwins as their best friends.)

Research also shows that adolescent twins, girls as well as boys, remain closer to their parents than singleton children, and that often they have a greater difficulty in rejecting their parents' values, especially if they've been reinforced by a cotwin throughout childhood. In other words, going against what Mom and Dad say means going against each other, too, and most multiples choose not to. In fact, two large studies done in Finland found that twins used alcohol and smoked less often than their single-born counterparts. The researchers, who tracked 284 twins from pregnancy through adolescence, concluded that the twin bond offered the support that these teens needed to say "no thanks" to dangerous behavior. Multiples, a peer group unto themselves, may find it easier to reject the questionable values of others. In addition, the twins in this study were found to be more physically active than their single-ton counterparts, participating in sports more often. Now how can you argue with all that good news?

We're in This Together

Let's go back to our own teenage years for just a minute. If you were like me, you probably spent hours yakking on the phone, hiding in the closet so your mom couldn't overhear the conversation. You exchanged notes with a close friend about what happened in school, who was seen kissing whom between classes, and on and on, ad nauseam. Every teen needs someone to talk to, to confide secrets both big and small. When you're a multiple developing simultaneously alongside a same-age sibling, you have someone who takes you seriously and understands what you're going through. While singletons turn to a close friend for this kind of support, most twins have that special relationship already built in. The strength of the twin bond helps to ease many teenage growing pains. This one positive component trumps all the other special challenges of being an adolescent twin.

The Popularity Factor

Many twins are great friends and take pleasure in being in each other's company. Their pool of friends is usually larger than that of singletons, too, as they share many acquaintances from each other's classes. Perhaps it's this strength of comradeship that draws others to them. In fact, studies reveal that being a preteen twin actually boosts a twin's popularity. In one study conducted over a five-year time span, more than 1,874 eleven- and twelve-year-old twin and nontwin classmates used the "peer nomination technique" to decide who in their classroom displayed socially active behavior—strong leadership abilities, being outgoing and popular, compliant behavior, and the ability to control emotions. The results? Twins surpassed singletons. In particular, opposite-sex twins, both male and female, exhibited stronger socially active behavior than single-born children.

While in Chapter 2 we saw how many young twins struggle more with social inhibitions and are less willing to play with unfamiliar peers than single-born youngsters, researchers believe that by the time they reach the age of twelve, many twins become more secure socially, perhaps due to their affiliation with a cotwin. They've had ample time to practice social skills since they're constantly exposed to a same-age peer, their cotwin. They have successfully learned to use this intratwin familiarity to enrich their social experiences outside the home.

While adolescent twins tend to be more socially adept and popular than their single-born counterparts, a study of nine- to seventeen-year-old twins found that relationships between multiples and their friends are less intimate than those of two single-born children. Perhaps the strong intratwin relationship prevents some multiples from developing "best friendships" with someone other than their cotwin. For many twins, their number one friend is still each other.

THE CHALLENGES OF BEING A TEENAGE MULTIPLE

Like all young teens, twins are forging their independence from their parents. (Some call adolescence the second separation.) But unlike their single-born friends, multiples have an added component—they're also trying to develop autonomy from their cotwin. In their early childhood, most multiples have acted as a team, but adolescence is a time to find new identities, shaking off the old labels of childhood. The outside world to a twin is getting bigger by the day. For many multiples, however, the idea of discovering the "I" rather than relying on the "we" is confusing and even somewhat scary. To further complicate matters, adolescent twins often look to their cotwins as a measure of their self-worth, and sometimes they don't like what they see. ("If you don't succeed or look good, then I don't either.") Many multiples think their cotwin is a reflection of themselves that constantly critiques achievements, social status, and yes, even emerging sexuality. It's no wonder adolescence is also a time when multiples opt in and out of the twin relationship—today I need you, tomorrow I won't—often out of sync with each other. Just when Twin A wants to hang out with his cotwin today, Twin B would rather go out alone with his buddy from science class. Next month, the roles are bound to shift again, where Twin B really wants to spend time with his brother, but Twin A just asked out the cute girl from his English class. It's this push-and-pull that can sometimes put a strain on the relationship.

Emerging Independence and Developing Autonomy

Most cultures value independence. Parents groom their young children to one day develop the ability to think and do for themselves, to become emotionally mature and independent. If all goes well, by the time kids reach their late teenage years, they will have learned to act more autonomously and at the same time seek out love and support from parents and peers when needed. Children need to learn autonomy, and parents need to give it to them. It's an important part of growing up and becoming an adult who has a healthy sense of self-esteem.

There are several types of autonomy, but here we'll focus on two—emotional and behavioral. Emotional autonomy deals with exploring personal feelings, focusing attention inwardly, and even seeking more privacy from one's family. (This is the time when teens love to sequester themselves in their bedrooms for hours!) This form of autonomy is the process of seeking more independence from parents by problem solving on one's own. Teens seek solutions by turning to outsiders (friends) rather than their parents for opinions and feedback. It's also the time when kids question the ideas and motives of their parents—they realize that their parents are fallible and not the superheroes they remember from early childhood.

Behavioral autonomy, on the other hand, is the ability to make personal everyday decisions—the ability to assess a situation, make a choice, and follow through with it. Teens realize that every decision has consequences and weigh their decisions accordingly. In this sense, multiples developing behavioral autonomy differ vastly from singleton children, since twins and higher-order multiples must base their decisions not only on what their parents think or say but also what their cotwins and cotriplets will think or say as well.

Growing autonomy means more individual decision making. Yet for multiples this growing autonomy is complicated, as they must take into account the added element of their cotwin. Every decision an individual multiple makes now has two components: approval or disapproval from one's parents *and* from one's cotwin. A perfect example is summer sleepaway camp. Let's say a fifteen-year-old twin has her heart set on going to a horseback riding camp for three weeks in the summer. Although her parents have given her permission, what will the reaction be of her cotwin? Should she ask her to go, too? What will be the cotwin's reaction if she isn't asked?

For some multiples, the quest for autonomy may be temporarily bumpy as each twin struggles to develop independence by detaching from the other. Although it may be upsetting to see your multiples' once-happy relationship on the skids as their bickering and fighting escalates to deafening proportions, realize that conflict is not only normal (and usually short-lived) but also necessary as they try to figure out their new roles as independent adults. For some twins, especially identical siblings, developing behavioral autonomy may take a bit longer as many MZ twins prefer to make joint decisions within the relationship.

The Big Separation

Unlike same-age, single-born children, who freely spend time away from the family, as young teens, many multiples haven't spent more than an afternoon away from their cotwin. Psychologist and author Mary Rosambeau surveyed six hundred twins and their parents in the United Kingdom and asked when the twins first spent two or more nights apart from each other. Compared to single-born children, who answered just shy of nine years old, the twins' average answer of fourteen and a half years old—more than a five-year difference—is rather eye opening. It's clear that twins, in general, don't have the same opportunities as single-born children to be alone. As a result, they don't always learn how to separate from one another. As young children, they learned to separate from their primary caregiver (Mom), but they did it alongside their twin. They may have gone to preschool, day care, or even an overnight visit to Grandma's house without Mom, but their twin was right there taking her place offering love and comfort. So by the time multiples reach age fourteen and begin spending more time away from their parents and cotwins, testing the waters of impending adulthood can be exciting and inhibiting at the same time. Adolescence, like early childhood, highlights many multiples' fears of separation.

When Separation Is Thrust Upon the Twinship. We've talked at length in Chapter 2 of the importance of encouraging independence at an early age. But what if a separation is forced upon multiples before either one is ready, such as when one twin requires an overnight hospital stay? It can often have a dramatic effect on twins, and not necessarily only on the patient. In a parent's effort to attend to the patient, the cotwin is often overlooked. He may be scared that his cotwin will not return and even jealous of the attention that his cotwin is receiving for her ailment. It's important for parents to remember that the healthy twin needs a bit of extra mothering as well.

When Separation Is Harder for One than the Other. Some twins may be ready to separate well before their cotwins. What if one twin experiments with change while the other remains content to stay within the confines of the twinship, one reveling in self-expression while the other holds tightly to his role as a cotwin? Although you should encourage your twin to spread his wings and fly on his own, if the other isn't ready for the separation, it can cause hurt feelings and friction between the pair. The twin who's not quite confident enough to be out on his own may experience feelings of rejection, of being left behind by his cotwin. He may actually grieve for what he sees as the breaking up of their twinship. Even though it's painful to watch one twin suffer, forcing the two to stay together is never a good idea and won't solve the problem. The twin who's ready to fly may feel stifled and obligated to his cotwin. If you hold one back for the sake of the other, you could further exacerbate a problem that would have eventually worked itself out.

Interestingly, research indicates that dominant twins, those who either take on the role of leader, the boss, or mother their cotwin, actually have a harder time with separation. When the passive twin is allowed to be on her own, free from the directions imposed on her by her cotwin, she actually blossoms and finds personal strength. The dominant twin, on the other hand, often doesn't understand why her cotwin wants independence (after all, the situation has worked out so well for the dominant twin) and has to forge a new identity for herself now that she is no longer in the caretaking role. It's then that the dominant twin can lose confidence and may need a bit of extra guidance to find new footing.

Fear not, though. Often when one multiple starts out on his own, whether it's starting to date, getting a part-time job, or even making new friends, it acts as a wake-up call to the other. If both twins take on change simultaneously, their relationship can remain equal and harmonious.

When New Friends Enter the Picture. Even by high school, many twins share the same friends or at least overlap many of the same acquaintances. Furthermore, many still count their cotwin as their closest buddy (MZ twins in particular). Yet children need to form intimate, trusting bonds with others outside of their families. Having a same-sex peer group during adolescence helps prevent isolation and anxiety, promotes positive self-esteem and confidence, and actually encourages individuation. When it comes to twins, though, the road to developing strong relationships with peers other than their cotwin has some twists and turns. Several empirical studies of adolescent twins, for instance, suggest that not only do many twins share the same friends but that they are often reluctant to go off with other kids if their cotwin is not otherwise engaged. Perhaps it's the guilt of leaving a cotwin behind—some multiples simply can't enjoy themselves if their sibling isn't bonded with another person. The researchers conclude that these children often have a harder time making outside social connections due to their close bond.

So what happens when one twin forms a new friendship before her cotwin does? If the twinship has been a close one, it can be extremely difficult for a new face to break into the group because one twin is bound to feel excluded and left out by the new relationship, and her cotwin may feel guiltily obligated to the twinship. Many budding outside friendships have been extinguished simply because the cotwin sees the new face as threatening to the twinship. Her twin may comply by letting the friendship die out in fear of hurting her sister's feelings by bonding with someone new.

Obviously if twins were brought up as "a pair" or if opportunities never existed in the home for individual experiences away from family and one's cotwin, they will have a harder time when new friends inevitably come onboard. It's in these extreme circumstances that twins often feel safer together than apart, a feeling that can persist into adulthood where both feel they cannot survive without the other. The key here for parents is to encourage individual expression and preferences as well as stressing respect for all family members.

Opposite-sex twins, on the other hand, who do not have to worry about competing for the same partners, actually have an

Dating Dilemmas and Delights

Being mistaken for your identical brother or sister may have been humorous when you were young. Who wouldn't have liked to play an April Fool's joke on the fourth-grade teacher by switching classrooms? But when MZ twins reach their teen years and interest in the opposite sex grows, it's anything but funny to be mistaken for one's cotwin. Now the focus is on individuality.

Parents of twins often worry about the day when same-sex twins pine after the same beau. Surprisingly, it rarely happens, as most twins abide by an unspoken system—they each deliberately choose different objects of their affection. It's as if they instinctively want to prevent a love triangle before it begins. Still, twins rarely keep their opinions of their cotwin's newest acquisition to themselves. Wanting only the best for her cotwin, a sister will undoubtedly point out the new beau's shortcomings more often than not.

added bonus—a larger dating pool. What could be less anxiety ridden than getting to know your twin's friends in the relaxed atmosphere of your own home with the safety of your family around? In fact, most boy-girl twins learn to be comfortable around the opposite sex sooner than their single-born counterparts because they have more exposure to the opposite sex. But if the female twin matures sooner than her brother and chooses to date an older boy, her date may treat her cotwin as her younger "kid" brother rather than her equal, which could cause some hard feelings between the pair.

So how can you help your multiples make their way through the dating maze? Strike up a "what if?" conversation with your multiples and encourage them to discuss a few ground rules between them such as, Is one ever allowed to date the other's ex-boyfriend or girlfriend? Are they ever open to double-dating?

Can they date their cotwin's best friend? What are the rules when opposite-sex twins have friends over—is it an open- or closed-door policy?

One mom explained another interesting dilemma that happened to her teenage boy-girl pair. "We all learned a funny story when they both did a Twin's Club panel of grown-up twins. They were talking about their high school experiences, and it came out that many girls were interested in meeting Michael (DZOSm) but didn't follow through because they thought that he was 'with that girl,' meaning his twin sister. Lesson to boy-girl twins: let others know that you are siblings!"

Off to College They Go. College is usually the first time most multiples go their separate ways. In fact, of the several parents that I interviewed who had college-age multiples, all

---

From One Parent to Another

"Victoria missed Michael (DZOS) tremendously for the five years that he served in the Marines. When he signed up, the Marines deferred him until after my birthday, but they decided to move up the date a week and a half. The recruiter called on a Monday to inform us that Michael had to report to St. Petersburg on Wednesday at 6 A.M. to ship out. I called Tori at work to let her know the details and suggested that she take off from work to spend some time with her brother. Her car pulled up in front of her house, followed by another. She had gotten so hysterical that her boss would not allow her to drive and had someone follow them to bring the boss back to the office. Michael and Victoria spent a lot of that time together, going back to their high school to visit with the teachers and the principal, and many other places that were dear to them. That Tuesday night she slept on his bed and he slept in a sleeping bag on the floor so that they could get every last bit of talking time together."

said going off to college was the first major separation for their pair. For some multiples, attending a university without one's cotwin is freeing as it's an opportunity to shed the "stigma" of twinship. For these multiples, the anonymity of college life allows them to explore new activities and subjects, make new friends, and embrace their newfound independence and individuality. But not every twin feels the need or desire to leave their twinship behind when they head off to school. In fact, it's not unusual for twins to attend the same college, especially MZ twins, who may want to study the same subjects and pursue the same careers. Even some DZ twins choose the same schools. They achieve parallel independence by living on opposite ends of campus.

Comparisons Often Escalate

When twins are young, most are unaware of the comparisons made about them. Some find the added attention exciting and flattering, even if it is in the form of a comparison from family, friends, and even strangers. Interestingly though, comparisons between twins actually increase as multiples get older, rather than diminish as one might expect. Especially for nonidentical twins (DZ), who may look and act nothing alike, comparisons of the differences between the pair are often exaggerated during adolescence as they grow and mature into individuals. These exaggerated comparisons can be a problem for adolescent twins who are just beginning to question their own personal identities. The constant comparisons between the pair's weight, height, and differences in abilities become an unwanted invasion of their privacy, an intrusion. The self-esteem of one or the other may suffer from these assessments, especially if one is a scholar and the other is struggling to keep his academic head above water, or if one twin feels he can

---

From One Parent to Another

"My sons are polar opposites of each other. The 'winter formal king' (DZSSm) is very outgoing and places a big emphasis on cultivating friendships. In college he is in a fraternity and spends his spring breaks on the beaches of Florida. My 'student government president' (DZSSm) is into academics and is student senate treasurer at his university and spends his spring breaks building houses for Habitat for Humanity and working with an environmental group to do parkland rehabilitation."

---

never truly measure up to his brother's athletic prowess. And what about physical appearance? It's so important to all teens, and twins are no exception. In the case of MZ twins where one may not take care of her personal appearance as well as the other would like, the more groomed twin often changes her look altogether so as not to be confused with her untidy sister. The outcome for some is a temporary breakup of the twinship as each struggles to get her personal footing.

Labeling at this stage is often used to distinguish between the two—one is called "the athlete" while the other assumes the tag of "the drama queen," for instance. Usually labeling in middle and high school revolves around scholastic achievement—one will undoubtedly gain the label of "the smart one" while the other is stuck with something not nearly as flattering.

Self-Esteem

We've already discussed how twins on average experience more learning problems than singletons, and when a twin reaches high school, the problem (especially if it was never addressed in elementary school) can continue to affect him in other ways, namely by diminishing his self-esteem. Researchers conclude that self-esteem has a direct relationship with school achievement. If children do well in school, they feel better about themselves. This is doubly true for twins. While singleton school performance is compared with the whole school population, twins are often compared to each other. Parents who continually put pressure on their less-achieving twin to keep up with his cotwin can compound the problem. It's important here to emphasize the need to forgo comparisons between twins. The danger lurks that the comparisons will become a self-fulfilling prophecy: if a twin has always felt like second to his or her twin, or less-than, then why bother trying to succeed as an adult? He or she will just come in second anyway. So what a twin believes is true, he will make come true.

Challenges for Parents

Adolescence often brings up issues from our childhoods. That's true for all kids, but for multiples some issues become amplified. For instance, issues of bonding sometimes resurface in the preteen years as some kids question their relationships with their moms and dads. Parents, too, are vulnerable to these feelings. Mom may feel guilty for how little time she was able to spend with each one as a baby and now gives in to her strong-willed teenage multiples to make up for her guilt. Or if she's never spent much time alone with each child individually during childhood, she may now feel she can't relate to either as they reach adulthood. By the time adolescence hits, some twins simply don't listen to their parents and instead team up with their cotwin to battle their point of view—a strong force to be sure.

What Parents Can Do

Yikes! Is being the parent of a teenage twin really that bad? Of course not. The past few pages merely point out difficulties that can arise—there's no guarantee that they will. If multiples have been encouraged throughout their lives to find their own unique path and identity and were raised in a home where family is valued, they have a much easier time dealing with typical teenage issues of self-worth when they reach adolescence. But just in case, here are a few ideas to help your children stay the course.

- If one multiple chooses to remain home after high school graduation and seems to be missing his cotwin, encourage him to try new things—study new subjects at a local community college, take up a new hobby, apply for an internship, even travel. Encourage him to take time to explore his own identity. Explain that the late teen years and early adult years are the perfect time to get to know what you truly want out of life.

- Encourage your twins to tolerate and respect each other's outside friendships. No rude behavior to someone the other does not like. Tell your multiples that everyone who steps foot in your home will be treated with respect.

- Recognize and acknowledge negative feelings between twins. If you allow your kids to vent, it often defuses the situation. (Obviously you can't allow vicious attacks—either physical or verbal—between siblings.) Try to stay out of their disagreements—don't cast judgment. Instead act as a sounding board and encourage them to work out their differences on their own. Give your twins the tools to deal with problems for themselves.

- Offer more time apart and allow for independent experiences. Arrange for each twin to spend the night at Grandma's alone. Encourage your multiples to attend a sleepaway camp or even apply for a part-time job. Never insist on twin togetherness by forcing one to take the other with him to a party, for instance. Let the twins decide for themselves how much time they wish to be together.

- Teens are acutely aware of their personal appearance. Don't compare multiples' looks to one another.
- Encourage individual goals and interests. Allow each child to find her own special niche in life. Allow for experimentation with new hobbies (art or music lessons), a different sport (your local community park usually offers many low-cost options), and academic pursuits (maybe your budding math whiz would like to join his school's math club).
- Keep issues of academic successes and disappointments separate. Never compare one twin to the other. The less comparisons are made both in the home and in the outside world, the more likely they'll have the freedom to choose and pursue their own goals—not ones forced upon them.
- Try to keep the lines of communication open. Pick non-stressful times for casual but candid conversations about teenage stress and pressure. (Car rides and family mealtimes are two good opportunities.) Once the conversation gets rolling, try to listen rather than "fix" the problem. Offer each multiple a separate ear, too, as they may not want to share everything with their cotwin.
- Understand that change and conflict are a normal part of the growing process. Acceptance and understanding go a long way to keeping the family peace. Relax rigid roles and allow for some mundane experimentation. (Will that purple hair really kill you?)
- Set limits. Don't let the power of two coerce or guilt you into changing the ground rules on curfews, chores, driving, and so on. Make each multiple accountable for her own actions. Don't punish both by taking away a special privilege (such as having the family car for the night) for an error in judgment by one.

Twin Coupling: Two to the End

Twins are born as a pair. New parents, in a constant state of exhaustion, unwittingly sanction this twin union by allowing their new babies to do everything together. When Dad changes one diaper, he changes the other. Both are put to bed at the same time regardless if one is ready while the other isn't. During the day, twins share the same playpen so they can amuse each other. We all did it. It's just the reality of life with young multiples.

And even as they grow and begin to develop distinct personalities, the world often continues to view twins as a pair, even if the family does not. People expect multiples to be alike and act alike and are confused if they don't look alike. The pressure many twins feel to conform to societal expectations can be strong. This coupling mentality will sometimes become embedded in the relationship and follow twins throughout their lives. It creates an enormous dilemma for them, too: on the one hand, twins feel the need to be seen individually, downplaying their twin status, yet they are and always will be identified as part of a pair.

The Couple Effect. Being born a pair affects twins' lives in many ways. Emotionally and psychologically tied to one another, twins essentially become part of one another. As a result, they act and react based on what the other does in the partnership. Noted psychologist Rene Zazzo calls this the couple effect. Zazzo believes that twins lose their individual identities and cultivate one expanded identity as a result of it. He doesn't see twins as identical, but rather as two intradependent beings.

The couple effect begins at birth. When multiples are little, they spend an enormous amount of time together. They quickly learn to count on one another for comfort and entertainment.

Since they have each other, they rely less on their parents than single-born children. Although the twin bond is special, it can isolate them, drawing them even closer together. While single-born children face many challenges solo, twins confront many of the same situations together, easing their hardship. When singletons go off to make new neighborhood friends, for instance, twins often venture out together. To make their partnership work more efficiently and avoid conflict, twins instinctively work as a team, taking on different, complementary roles, or they each specialize in a separate area. The upside to this division of labor is the strength and power that the couple feels together. But, Zazzo says, they lose their individuality in the process. These roles can become so imbedded within the partnership that neither gets the chance to freely explore the roles or tasks of the other. The couple effect, therefore, masks who each multiple really is. (Research has shown that when twins grow up separately, free from the couple effect, they actually exhibit many similarities to each other. Heredity takes over as their natural, innate tendency to be alike surfaces, sometimes making twins raised separately more similar than those raised together.) In extreme cases, some twins become tremendously dependent on each other and have trouble forming other relationships. Some will never venture into unknown pursuits without the comfort of having their cotwin by their side.

Many parents may find the couple effect theory hard to digest, since most twins don't exhibit these characteristics to that great extent. Yet if you observe them carefully, you may see subtle signs of the couple effect in your own multiples. I see some with my own kids. For instance, my boys are in the same fourth-grade class this year. This is the first time they've been together since preschool. One son keeps forgetting his homework and relies on his cotwin to fill him in at night. The forgetful son—a good student, mind you—never did this when he was in class by himself, but in the first five months of this school year, he's neglected to write down his assignments six times. Why? Because his cotwin has phenomenal memory—he's the kind of kid who can hear a story once and repeat it back word for word—this son subconsciously allows his brother to take on the task.

When twins reach the teen years, the couple effect often becomes more pronounced. With the need to be seen as different and unique, multiples often exaggerate their opposite roles. Once best friends and confidants, twins suddenly seem at odds with each other. Even if they share similar interests, some twins deliberately choose different school subjects, sports, or activities than their cotwin merely for the sake of establishing their own unique identity. They fall over each other trying to be different, stressing that they are not the same. They become extreme opposites: One may dress like a punk rocker because his cotwin prefers to dress conservatively. One twin feels he can't be "the honor roll student," too, because his cotwin already took that position. Instead, he takes on the role of rebel. Trying to maintain these roles puts an extreme amount of stress on teenage multiples—the high achiever strives for perfection in everything he does, while the "bad boy" sets himself up to continually fail, his self-esteem deteriorating in the process. Researchers find that this happens more often when twins are the only children in the family or when parents have overemphasized their twinship.

The Prima Donna Effect. As children, many identical

From One Parent to Another

"We wonder all the time what Sheila's and Virginia's (DZSSf) personalities would have been if they didn't have the other there to push them away from what they were doing. They tried to be opposites on purpose. You wonder what they would have turned into if they developed alone."

females (and some nonidentical females as well) enjoy being seen as special and different. They revel in their twinness and because of it often interact very easily with other children and adults. Yet as twins reach the teen years, the novelty of "seeing double" often fades as many new peers reach out to each twin individually. Many kids may not even realize that the girl they sit next to in science class, for instance, is actually a twin. Now more than ever, multiples need to have individual social skills to make it on their own. Sadly, some lack this ability to make and keep friends individually. For their entire lives being known as a twin—being part of a team—has been their social platform, their identity. Now some may find it difficult and maybe even a bit frightening to make it socially on their own. With the twin-attention gone, their self-esteem suffers, their confidence fades, and they become anxious.

It's at this point that some twins, MZ girls in particular, build upon their similarities, almost clinging to their twinness, as a way to increase their popularity. They try to fabricate the illusion of likeness even more than their genes would suggest. Girls who continue to dress alike through the middle and high school years may be relying on their twinship for social survival. Psychologist Helen Koch coined this the prima donna effect. Often parents have unwittingly reinforced the prima donna effect by giving both MZ and DZ females alliterative names (Kathy and Karen, Sarah and Susan), encouraging their daughters to dress alike for special occasions where they would be noticed and admired by many, or simply treating them more alike than they would any other offspring.

The prima donna effect can affect twin girls' sense of autonomy, too. One study found that adolescent identical twin girls believed that their intradependence wasn't a problem. The study further indicated that as these girls' popularity increased, their individuation decreased—the girls succumb to the peer pressure of being seen as a popular duo at the expense of their own separate individuality.

THE TWIN BODY

Take a look at any fifth- through seventh-grade class, and what do you see? Kids of all heights, sizes, and levels of development. Some girls look as though they're on the brink of adulthood (some a little too adult perhaps), while their female classmates still look like little girls. The boys are no different. Some are tall with deep voices, while their classmates could still try out for the Vienna Boys' Choir. The point here is that, as everyone knows, puberty hits everyone at a different time—biology is rarely in sync with chronology. And girls, on average, reach puberty earlier than boys. They reach their peak rate of growth a whopping two years earlier than boys.

This would be a no-brainer for most parents and kids to accept. Yet for twins, it sometimes can prove to be a bit more problematic.

Differences in Growth

For multiples, pubertal growth patterns vary by zygosity. For instance, MZ twins who share the exact same genetic makeup are usually very similar in their growth patterns—both weight and height—during puberty. Even if they varied greatly in size at birth, they often catch up with each other throughout childhood and accordingly hit pubertal stages almost concurrently. In fact, in the case of MZ girls, many will start menstruation within days of each other (although it's not uncommon for the gap to span three to six months).

DZ multiples, on the other hand, who share only 50 percent of their DNA, are simply siblings born on the same day. The

differences in their growth patterns as well as when they hit
puberty will fluctuate just as it
does with any other single-born
brothers and sisters. DZ girls, for
example, can begin their periods
in tandem, but more often than
not the difference in timing can
be longer—up to several years—
since the normal range for
female menstruation is anywhere
between the ages of ten and sev-
enteen. (But try telling that to

> **From One Parent to Another**
>
> "Virginia (DZSSf) reached puberty a year and a half before Sheila (DZSSf). We pointed out to Sheila that she got to do many things first and that now it was Virginia's turn. Yet when Sheila hit puberty, she knew what to do; she was well versed and prepared. They must have discussed it between them."

your daughter as she laments that her cotwin is now a "woman" while she is still a little girl.) And what about the female figure? In a society where so much emphasis is placed on a young woman's bra size, it can be brutal for multiples when one is much larger or smaller than her cotwin.

While girls focus mostly on their figures and the arrival of their periods, boys, on the other hand, concentrate on height differences. To many DZ male twins, being shorter than the rest of your classmates is bad enough, but to have your twin brother tower over you by several inches hurts all the more. Insensitive family members and even friends who feel the need to point out the difference at every picnic or gathering often compound the shorter twin's feelings of insecurity. Yet a large difference in height is the norm when one boy begins puberty months ahead of his twin brother. The problem is further exas-perated if the former is heavier than his twin since thinner children start puberty later.

Same-sex twins may experience a few bumps in the road when each is entering puberty at a different time, but nowhere is the varying onset of puberty more evident than with opposite-

---

From One Parent to Another

"Genna (DZOSf) reached puberty several years before Nathan (DZOSm). For a number of years they were developmentally very far apart and seemed more like an older sister and younger brother. He was pretty sad at age ten when his 'buddy' didn't want to have anything to do with him and treated him like an annoying little kid. We tried to help Nathan by explaining that boys and girls grow up on different schedules and a time would come when they'd be friendlier again. It wasn't a serious problem because this was when Nathan began to travel for his ski racing, and he soon had other distractions. Around age fifteen, he caught up and they became closer."

---

sex pairs. At no other time is the relationship of boy-girl twin sets tested as much as in puberty. As stated previously, girls on average begin puberty up to two years before boys. (In fact, even at birth twin girls are ahead of their brothers biologically by one-and-one-half months.) We have seen that little girls are socially more advanced than little boys in language and reading skills, too. Now when an adolescent male is just beginning to identify strongly with all things manly, he is literally overshadowed by his twin sister. In a society where height is considered a sign of masculinity, a male twin's ego and self-image can be beaten down if his sister stands several inches taller than he. Already more socially aware, she has the heads-up on dealing with the opposite sex. She may no longer want to hang out with her brother and will instead choose dates several years older than her cotwin. To feel more comfortable in the dating pool, the male twin may choose dates younger than he. The resulting gap between her date's age and his date's age could be several years—not exactly the perfect setup for a double date. In addition, girls on the brink of puberty crave more privacy, while often their twin brothers couldn't care less about it. She may want more private time with mom to discuss girl things, while he's content to live his life as an open book.

Much of this teen angst is merely a transient problem since it usually all works out once twins reach adulthood. So fear not, boys do catch up to their sisters—and usually end up about five inches taller on average. And often even the late bloomer will catch up to his cotwin, sometimes even surpassing him. Most single-born siblings would barely notice this simple reality of nature, yet for many twins it's a time of discontent in their relationship. For those who develop much later than their cotwins, it's a source of anxiety and embarrassment. Some may lack confidence and suffer from low self-esteem. Bouts of frustration coupled with moodiness (and even hostility) surface. Family members may have higher expectations of the more mature twin; the slower-developing twin may have strong feelings of resentment and try to gain attention in other, more unsavory ways.

What Parents Can Do

Although it may seem like adolescent kids wouldn't be caught dead snuggling up with Mom or Dad, that's exactly what many of them need right now. Parents can help offset some of the anxieties their twins feel about their bodies simply by spending more time with them and just listening. Below are a couple of other ideas to help ease twins' worries.

- Parental reassurance that everything is just fine goes a long way. Perhaps relating a similar tale of when you were a young teen will help alleviate his anxiety. Or, if your twin would prefer, why not schedule a physical with his pediatrician? The expert opinion and support from an outside party may just do the trick.

- Be aware of the fact that twins assess their body as it compares to their cotwin's and swiftly step in if it takes an unhealthy turn. This is especially dangerous with girls. If one twin is a few pounds less than her twin sister, and the latter girl begins a diet to lose a few pounds more, the first sister may feel compelled to lose even more weight to regain her slight edge over her sister.
- In opposite-sex pairs where the boy is lagging behind his sister in maturity, a strong father-son relationship (or any close male friend or relative that can act as a father figure and confidant) is an enormous boost to the boy's confidence right now. Keep him busy, too, with hobbies, sports, and even a part-time job. Consider an all-boys school where he can shine on his own and learn how to be independent. By the same token, girls need their parents' acceptance that they are growing up. Mother-daughter outings are a wonderful way of reaffirming and celebrating this stage in life.
- If differences are great, allowing for more personal privacy is often beneficial for both parties, especially for opposite-sex multiples.

From One Parent to Another

"In the early teens Victoria (DZOSf) tended to want to be alone in her room to preen and pose and dance in front of the mirror. Her brother (DZOSm), if he wanted to share something, had a tendency to barge in and catch her in embarrassing moments, even if only to her, and they would fight. It took a lot more of retraining to knock on doors and wait to be asked in. Of course, when she wanted something she, too, was known to barge into his room and then could not understand why he was upset. I still have the cracks in the doors to remind me."

- If your MZ twins experience a prolonged, marked difference in their growth, a trip to the doctor is in order to make sure they're each developing as they should be.

TWO TIMES THE HORMONES AND TWO TIMES THE FUN

Adolescence can be a challenging time for many families with multiples, especially for their parents. Yet when an adolescent has a cotwin by his or her side, it helps make the road a bit smoother, even if the relationship at times seems anything but. The goal here is for twins and higher-order multiples to reach adolescence on a path of their own choosing—the problems surface when they're on identical roads and then suddenly feel that they must force themselves to take different exits.

8

Family Relationships: Mom, Dad, and the Single-Born Siblings

As I continue with my research on intratwin relationships day after day, something continues to lurk in the back of my mind, nagging for equal attention. It's something that I keep missing. It's my youngest son. He's not a twin, but rather a single-born child who arrived on the scene exactly two and a half years after his twin brothers. Obviously he's a huge part of our family dynamics—his booming personality would never let us over-look that fact. But I realize that all the attention I've placed on raising multiples—scrutinizing the right way to parent them and the special challenges they face—may be at his expense. Perhaps you've felt it too while reading this text. All this infor-mation on multiples is great, you think, but what about the other children in the family? They have special needs as well. Don't they count too? Absolutely. In fact, here's a whole chap-ter devoted to them.

Being a singleton in a family with multiples is different than being in a family with all single-born children. For starters, the older singleton has to quickly get used to taking a backseat to her younger "celebrity" siblings, especially when the twins are young and constantly together. Younger singletons face hurdles, too, as their older twin or even triplet siblings often present a united front, way too powerful for one child to easily infiltrate.

In this chapter, we'll talk about ways that you can help your older or younger single-born child build a stronger relationship with each twin. Multiples are a close-knit group, but that doesn't mean they can't have that kind of bond with other siblings as well.

FAMILY DYNAMICS 101

In every family there are two separate groups: the parent dyad and the sibling group. When twins or triplets enter the picture, a third dyad (or triad or quad) forms—the multiple group. Never underestimate the effects the twin dyad can have on a family! They may be little, but they can be powerful. At one end of the spectrum, they can become a commanding force exerting an enormous amount of pressure on the family to join in their point of view, or at the very least, stand strong together when other family members oppose them. Fortunately for most families, the twin dyad usually just creates a mild disturbance for parents, though it certainly keeps them on their toes.

Since identical (MZ) twins share the closest relationship of all multiple subgroups, they often act in concert, exerting more power in the family than just two single siblings or even nonidentical (DZ) twins. Instinctively banding together, they'll sometimes try their hand at undermining their parents. ("Well, Dad said it was fine if we wanted to stay out past eleven.") By presenting a united front, parents balance out this strong twin dyad, foiling their plans of world domination. And Mom and Dad should absolutely act in concert with one another since strong parent solidarity is paramount in families with multiples.

Kids are smart, and if they even suspect a hint of conflicting parenting style, they'll try to use it to their advantage. Although all kids would do this, twins have the extra power play of working as a team. They know it, and they'll use it whenever it's to their advantage.

Should the parent dyad disintegrate, the consequences are far-reaching. If one parent tries to align herself with the twin dyad, for instance, such as a mother who always acts and reacts on the behalf of her twin daughters, the other parent is sure to feel excluded, ultimately straining the marriage. And what happens in single-parent homes? Often when the family unit breaks down either through separation, divorce, or death, the twin dyad usually remains intact and often becomes even stronger. The pair may recede into their own little group as a way of protecting themselves, offering support and a sense of safety to each other, while possibly excluding their single-born siblings. This is true with MZ twins in particular.

All these forces—the interactions between cotwins themselves and how they relate to others within the family—have a great influence on each twin's developing personality as well as on their siblings.

Help for Single-Parent Families

I bet you never thought you'd be the parent of twins or triplets, but now here you are the single parent of multiples and possibly other single-born children. You're not alone—families with multiples have a higher rate of divorce than those with single-born children. While the stress for caring for multiples is often palpable, especially in the first few years, doing it solo can be twice as overwhelming. So how can you keep it all together?

(continued on next page)

Help for Single-Parent Families *(continued)*

- Admit you need help and then find it any way you can. You have several options: If your multiples are young and you have the room in your home, you may want to consider taking in a college student as a boarder in exchange for nanny services and light housekeeping. Some single parents of twins have chosen to move back home with their parents or at least nearby—the loving support of family, whether emotional or financial, has helped many parents of twins cope better. If moving back home is not in the cards, consider soliciting the help of willing friends who'd like to come over to lend a hand once a week. At the very least the adult conversation will nurture you for the week ahead.
- Reach out for emotional support. These days, support groups come in all shapes and sizes to meet everyone's lifestyle. Join your local Mothers of Twins Club (nomotc.org) or a single-parent group where others in the same situation can offer mutual support. If you'd prefer, you can connect to others online through message boards such as the one for single parents at *Twins* magazine (go to twinsmagazine.com and click on "message boards") or speak privately with a professional counselor either in person, through e-mail, or even over the telephone at Twinsight (twinsight.com) or Twin Services (twinservices.org).
- Tune in to your children's emotional health, too. If the children's father or mother is deceased or has chosen to step out of the picture altogether leaving a void in your young children's lives, consider signing the kids up for Big Brothers Big Sisters (bbbs.org), the largest mentoring organization in the United States.
- Develop a daily routine. It may sound simple, but a family functions better when everyone knows what to expect day in and day out. Write up a day-to-day family schedule noting where everyone is and hang it where everyone can see. Include daily chores for all children, even the

Help for Single-Parent Families *(continued)*

youngest. You'd be amazed at how kids will rise to the occasion and follow along. By getting the kids involved and teaching them how to do for themselves you'll not only bring the family closer together, but your stress level is sure to decrease as well.

- Take time for yourself. Make exercise a priority in your life (it's a natural stress reliever) and get out at least once a month to visit with close friends.
- Be optimistic. Fill your life with positive affirmations and take the time to enjoy your beautiful children. Their smiles can make any day seem a little better.

Multiples and Birth Order

We've all heard lots about sibling birth order and its effects on the family—the oldest is the most serious, the high achiever of the family; the middle child is the mediator and often feels his or her position isn't as respected as the older or younger; the youngest is the free spirit, the spoiled one. In some families, multiples can also put a special spin on the dynamics. For instance, when DZ twins are the oldest in a family, a little power struggle can develop between the two as each wants to be seen as the oldest, the boss. Most of the time, it's relatively harmless and more of an annoyance than anything else. If one says, "When Mom goes out today, I'm in charge," the other is sure to counter with, "No you're not! I am." (MZ twins, because of their shared DNA, often work together rather than against each other.)

There is some good news if twins are the middle children, however. They often don't feel as excluded as their single-born counterparts since twins have an understanding partner who knows exactly how they feel. Once again, in times of stress

From One Parent to Another

"Kate and Victoria's (MZf) relationship with their older single-born sister is a bit tougher at times. When they try to gang up on Audra [older single-born daughter], we come down pretty hard on them. We are so blessed with Audra's disposition—she is such a caring, nurturing, forgiving person. We don't ever let them take advantage of her generosity, however. And since Victoria and Kate are in middle school now, they go to her for advice and support as a big sister who has been there. They talk about fashion, what to put in their lockers, teachers, boys, and whatever. This is the best thing."

these twins can retreat and find solace within each other.

In most families with three singleton children, two siblings eventually pair up and become more involved in each other's lives, leaving the third as the odd man out. In a family with three children including twins, however, a younger or older sibling can dilute the twin relationship, pairing up with one, then the other at different times, but often the intratwin bond remains the strongest. MZf (identical females) in particular can sometimes be especially critical of younger or older siblings, forcing the singleton to distance himself or herself from the family. In twin families with four children, two sets of dyads often form—the twins acting as one, the other two children forming the other. In five-child families—with or without twins—one child undoubtedly has to fend for herself. This child, whether older or younger, needs continual guidance, reassurance, and understanding from Mom and Dad as he or she tries to find a comfortable position in the family's hierarchy.

Families with triplets should proceed with caution, too, making sure that two of the three don't take the "oldest" and "youngest" roles, leaving the third multiple to question his position in the family and then seek attention in other more negative ways. One mom with a set of triplets, two identical girls and one fraternal girl, related how she lovingly handled the situation early on when her nonidentical daughter realized that she was not like her sisters. "The identical girls are brunettes, while the fraternal girl is a blonde. When they were four years old, Kristy, my blonde, was looking at a picture of all of them when they were one year old. Now she was looking at it very intently with a really sad face, so I asked her what was wrong. She looked up at me and asked why she didn't look like her sisters," the mom explained. She told her daughter that God knew she couldn't take another Kelly and Kerry, so he gave her Kristy. Satisfied with the answer, Kristy just smiled and went on to the business of playing. This mom tried often to help her daughter realize how special she was.

Interestingly enough, age has little to do with all these relationships. It seems that the need to be bonded or attached with another sibling takes precedence over the age of the sibling.

THE SIBLINGS

The other day, I sat back and just observed my three sons at play in my living room. It was pretty loud (as it usually is around here) as each made up and acted out a silly story complete with sound effects. Although they

---

From One Parent to Another

"Actually the real strain in our family has been Emily's [older, single-born daughter] relationship with her siblings. She was so young when she had to share her parents with not one but two intruders. She used to call them by one name. Her favorite saying when guarding her toys from Julie and Kevin (DZOS) was, 'No, Dooleytev!' They are very close in age, that's both a blessing and a curse. We say that any two of them do well together, it's the threesome that sometimes spells trouble. Actually, Emily is getting more mature, and that somewhat helps. We feel optimistic that they will continue to care about and for each other."

were driving me a little nuts, I couldn't help but think they were creating priceless memories as brothers that they'd recount to their own kids some day.

The sibling bond is the most powerful of all. My sons' relationships with each other will be the longest of any they have—longer than their relationship with their father and me, longer than their own marriages, and even longer than the relationships they will have with their own kids.

On a very simplistic level, having siblings offers free, unending entertainment. Even on the most boring of days, there's always someone to play with. Furthermore, experts say that the sibling bond expands each child's cognitive abilities, spurs the imagination, teaches cooperation, builds self-confidence, and helps to hone social skills. Not bad. As a bonus, research suggests that the more same-sex, close-in-age siblings twins have, the easier it is for the pair to adequately develop a strong sense of individual identity, which some twins struggle with.

Being the single-born sibling of a set of twins or triplets has its challenges, though. For instance, I've often heard my youngest son trying to convince his older twin brothers that they are in fact triplets. (He loves it when strangers ask if the three of them are.) Of course his claim is immediately met with scoffs and dismissals, but he argues his case nonetheless. To me he's simply trying to say that he wants to be part of their special alliance—he wants to be included in their special twin club. He senses their close connection and envies it.

Whether a child is younger or older than her twin siblings makes a difference in her plight as well. The older sibling sometimes feels upstaged by the arrival of multiples, while the younger often feels locked out as the pair already have a playmate in each other. Yet as you'll read further, you'll understand that these dynamics don't have to be permanent or detrimental to the sibling relationships.

The Older Sibling

It's not all bad news for an older sibling of multiples. In fact, there are lots of benefits. First of all, older singletons on average become more self-reliant—a trait that benefits them throughout their lives. If Mom is busy attending to infant twins, for example, the single sibling may have to fetch her own cookies and milk rather than relying on Mom to do it. After the arrival of twins, many single siblings actually develop a closer relationship with their parents. Perhaps it's because parents feel sympathetic toward their nontwin children or that's it's easier to bond with a single child since connecting to two infants at once takes a bit more time. Parents who had a singleton before the arrival of twins often told me that their oldest child was a great helper, and many couldn't have managed without the singleton's aid. One mom whose husband traveled for business said it was her older son who took care of her during those early twin years. If she fell asleep on the sofa while nursing the twins, for instance, he'd wake her to tell her it was time for bed—and he was only seven years old at the time. Because of this special

> ### From One Parent to Another
>
> "Kaitlyn is two years older than Ally and Beth (MZf). I think they have a wonderful relationship and always have. Katie is a very outgoing and friendly child—she made sure when people were asking about the twins that they knew she was the older sister. It's funny, but she didn't have a problem telling them apart until they were about four years old. She would look at whoever was near her and say, 'Say something,' because she could tell their voices apart. That only lasted for a short time, and now she has no problem telling them apart. Katie sees herself as the educator and protector. She's the almighty in her own eyes and doesn't like it when the twins tell her that she is not their boss. Over the years Katie has learned to let them have their own opinions, and their relationship is awesome."

From One Parent to Another

"When Andrew and Jeffrey (DZSSm) were born, Rob [older, single-born son] got a little rebellious. He had been an only child for six years. He wanted a brother or sister so bad and then came Joey, and Rob was thrilled. But then eleven months later, there were two more of them! I know Rob was overwhelmed. He acted out in school, but he eventually settled down and became the big brother. He was my right hand."

kind of mother-child relationship, many of the moms continue to feel a profound closeness to their eldest, single-born child.

Research also shows that the more single-born children there are in a family before the arrival of twins, the better the family as a whole functions, since the singletons form close-knit relationships with each other (that sibling dyad or group we talked about). And finally, older children tend to take a more active role in the care and raising of multiples than they do singleton babies. Older siblings often become teachers and mentors in the eyes of their younger siblings.

Yet a few problems can surface in families with multiples and older singleton children. When twins come along, so much care and attention is inevitably showered on the new multiples that some older children feel that they get much less consideration from both their parents and outsiders, especially if they are several years older than their multiple siblings. For these kids, it's a big adjustment learning to share the love of Mom and Dad. One study found that attention-getting behavior sometimes resurfaces temporarily in older, single-born children such as bed-wetting and reverting to baby talk. That's where grandparents and other extended family members can step in to help. When a loving volunteer gives a bit of her undivided time and attention to the older single sibling, Mom and Dad can attend to the innumerable demands of infant multiples without feeling guilty. And it's easier for outside family mem-

---

From One Parent to Another

"Emily [younger, single-born daughter] loves her big sisters (MZf) and looks up to them. In fact, we have nicknamed her 'The Emulator.' But there is a five-year age difference, and she will always be in a different phase from them, will always have different needs, will always be just a little bit left out as compared to their relationship with each other and the things they do together. I almost feel bad for her that they have a relationship that she does not. I have sometimes pondered if the relationships would be different if the age gap were smaller, or if the genders were different (boy singleton, or boy-girl twins and a singleton). But it is what it is. I don't think she's any worse the wear for it—she's a happy and well-adjusted child. But I wonder as she grows up if she will always feel a little left out."

---

bers to pick up the slack with an older sibling rather than trying to learn the nuances of bottle-feeding newborn twins. Still, parents need to walk a fine line between caring for young multiples and ensuring that the single-born child doesn't feel like he or she's being pushed aside.

Parents also need to be careful that they don't always assume their singleton would rather be out and about with Grandma than home with his new siblings. Some singleton children relish the time they spend with their multiple siblings and develop deep, meaningful bonds with them. In one study of triplet families, for example, the older singleton bonded with the multiple that was the same sex while the other two same-sex triplets grew close. In this particular case, the family created two close sibling dyads, instinctively avoiding leaving one child out.

The twins' zygosity plays a role in the twin-singleton relationship, too. Studies indicate that older siblings showed more resentment toward MZ twins than DZ twins, perhaps jealous

---

From One Parent to Another

"Kevin and Shane (DZSSm) have always been close. I never felt the need to entertain them as much as I do their sister. I think that with the boys being older than my daughter it's easier than having it the other way around—they've always shared my attention, and so when she was born they weren't very affected by it. She was never resented because she took me away from them."

---

of their inherently close bond. And not surprisingly, older male singletons have a harder time than older females in connecting with their new multiple brothers or sisters. Little girls usually enjoy the role of big sister and savor the added attention that twins bring. It sometimes takes a little longer for boys to warm up to their role as big brother. Over time, however, most older siblings get the hang of the new family dynamics and adapt just fine.

The Younger Sibling

When a single-born baby arrives after twins or triplets, the good news is that Mom and Dad have it all figured out and caring for one seems like a breeze. One diaper instead of two? Piece of cake. One bottle to warm instead of a trio? No problem. In fact, parents could probably care for a solo infant with their eyes closed—although it's not recommended. The multiples themselves seem to adjust better to the new bundle of joy than do single-born siblings, since twins occupy each other while Mom or Dad is busy attending to the needs of the newborn. (Most multiples don't demand that the new baby return to the hospital where he came from, for instance.) Plus, they're used to sharing the love and attention of their parents since they've always shared it with each other.

> **From One Parent to Another**
>
> "Heather and Holly (MZf) got a lot of attention by virtue of the fact that they were twins and that they were the first grandchildren. I remember we were out to dinner one day with my father-in-law, and one of his friends walked up. My father-in-law said, 'These are my grand-daughters, Heather and Holly.' Hailey [younger, single-born daughter] was sitting right next to them, and he never introduced her! It has been very difficult to the point where when Hailey was about eleven years old, she would take books with her when the family all went out to dinner. She'd sit at the other end of the table and read in spite of my efforts to try to draw her in. Only recently has she begun to come out of it. When the girls graduated from UCLA, Holly went to Denver to get her master's. This was the turning point in the relationship with Heather and Hailey—they became close because Holly was essentially out of the picture. Then Holly came home and Heather started to prepare for the bar exam. During this time, Holly and Hailey got close since Heather was pretty much locked up in a law library."

The honeymoon may end, though, when a younger, single-born sibling grows into a preschooler and slowly figures out what he's up against. Younger, single-born children will often resort to negative attention-seeking behavior as they feel it's the only way to get what they need. In our house, for instance, my younger singleton immediately reverts to screaming (we're talking loud) when he wants something from his older brothers. He feels they're not listening to him, and he thinks yelling will do the trick. Since that rarely works, he gives up and then quickly turns to crying in the hope that I'll rescue him. He feels helpless against them, and his frustration is often tangible. And this frequently happens for seemingly innocent disagreements—what to watch on TV, a coveted Lego piece, or even losing in a game, for instance.

What Parents Can Do

Parents can help single-born children develop close-knit relationships with their multiple siblings. So turn up your parenting antennae, watch for your cues, play up the positive, and read on.

- Downplay birth order in twins and single-born children. Never refer to the firstborn twin as the oldest and the second as the youngest. Allow each twin and their single-born siblings the opportunity to go first. Don't focus solely on just the oldest. Mix up the birth order when signing the family holiday card, choosing the weekend video, playing games, or even referring to them to others.
- Downplay the twin status especially when out in public. When someone asks, "Are they twins?" have a "script" or a quick, automatic response. "Yes, and this is their big sister. She's a wonderful role model for them." Never give special privileges to twins and not the other siblings just because the former were born together.
- Help the older single sibling feel special in her role as older sister by giving special, exclusive privileges such as staying up later or receiving a higher allowance.

From One Parent to Another

"My daughter [older singleton] didn't want one brother, much less two, even though she was only a toddler when they were born. She was very jealous of the attention Karsen and Kaden (MZm) demanded. Many people would speak to us about the babies and leave her out, so we had to compliment her as being a great helper and big sister. This helped a lot, and she is more of a friend to them now. She would still rather have a sister though!"

- Help the younger sibling see that her role in the family is just as important by making alone-time just for her.
- Discourage the gang mentality—twins against singleton—by deterring your twins from speaking as "we." Instead encourage each of them to use the word "I" when talking to single-born siblings. Don't speak about the twins as a pair, but rather use each of their names to stress that they are two individual members of the family.
- Ignore negative attention-seeking behavior from single-born children such as tattling, shouting, and arguing. Reward positive behavior such as cooperation, sharing, and compassion.
- Foster the relationships between your singleton and multiples. Swap roommates among all siblings regularly rather than having the twins bunk together exclusively. Encourage the older members of the family to mentor the younger ones. Regularly take one twin and one singleton sibling out for a special day to help build their connection or find something that the singleton has in common with each of

---

From One Parent to Another

"Rebecca [younger, single-born daughter] is developmentally advanced, especially socially, and Gabriel and Jordan (MZm) are developmentally behind, especially socially, so they kind of meet up in the middle. They are big playmates; they really love each other. Sometimes she feels left out, especially in the beginning. Way back, it was hard for my husband and me to incorporate her—it took a while to remember that we now had three kids. There were a couple of times when we got something for the boys and we didn't get something for Rebecca, or we planned something and didn't include her. She's now hypervigilant about not being excluded from anything. She has really exerted her presence."

her multiple siblings and encourage them to explore their interests together.

THE PARENTS

Although it's still some nine years away, I sometimes think about when my twins will leave for college or move out on their own. It's painful for me to envision (where's my hankie?) since more than likely they will both leave at the same time, unlike single-born children who leave one by one over the course of several years. Just as immediately as the day they came into the world and I was thrust into learning to care for two at once, when my twins fly the nest, my heart will break twice.

A Different Bonding Experience

When my third son came along, I quickly realized that the early mothering and bonding experience was completely different than it was with my twins. While I did my best when my twins were babies to spend time alone with each one just cuddling and gazing into each child's eyes, there was always someone waiting in the wings to have me do exactly the same to him. With my single-born son, however, all my gazing and cooing could be devoted to him and him alone. That's one of the most significant and poignant differences between the mother-singleton and mother-multiple relationships. Mothers of multiples have to fight for some of the intimacy that mothers of singletons take for granted.

When you have several children of different ages, they're all at different stages, too. When your son goes off to preschool for the day, you're then free to devote yourself completely to his baby sister. Or when the baby sister is taking her nap, you're then available to read to her preschool brother. You can freely relate to each child one-on-one. Mothers of multiples, on the other hand, have to often interact with both their twins at once. Furthermore, when you have twins you have to deal with the multiple dyad—the twin bond— from which you are excluded, something that moms with single-born children don't have to contend with. This isn't meant to imply that your relationship with your twins or triplets is marred or lesser in any way simply because you had more than one child at a time, I'm merely pointing out that when you have multiples you have to be a bit more aware of the relationship and a bit more inventive in finding ways to develop that intimate bond with each of your children.

> **From One Parent to Another**
>
> "Julie and Kevin (DZOS) joined their seventeen-month-old sister Emily, and then we became a family of five. I found it hard to get who Julie and Kevin were as infants—it was a lot harder to bond with them individually than it had been with Emily. I remember nursing them individually and trying to figure out just who they were."

Yet many twins have a much stronger relationship with their father than do single-born children. Why, you ask? One good theory is that fathers of twins were thrown into the role of caretaker, even if in the beginning they would have preferred to stay on the sidelines. Although times are slowly changing, Mom still assumes the role of primary caretaker while Dad plays the supporting role. In families with twins or triplets, however, Dad gets into the act much sooner and to a greater degree. Immediately following the birth of their multiples, dads have to quickly learn how to diaper and bottle-feed, bathe and comfort his brood. Because of this many dads of twins bond much quicker with their children than a father with a single-born child.

The good news for Dad and his children radiates even further; because of his strong association with his multiples, some of the more challenging aspects of the twin situation are balanced out. For instance, constant paternal presence and caretaking contributes to a twin's sense of autonomy—his personal identity. Also, studies have shown that a father's early involvement in his children's care facilitates a stronger sense of sexual identity in his kids.

Fighting Feelings of Isolation

Since moms of multiples have different mothering experiences than moms of single-born children, the mom of multiples may feel somewhat isolated. Where mothers of singletons can reach out to a large group of women who are in the same circumstances, the mother of multiples has to search to find such support. That's why groups such as the National Organization of Mothers of Twins Clubs (nomotc.org) are invaluable resources. Members are women who are in the same circumstances as you. Monthly meetings usually feature guest speakers, often parenting professionals who are familiar with parenting twins. Often the groups host family outings as well as Mom's night out. With more than 475 groups nationwide, you're sure to find a local group nearby. (Many of the moms I spoke with said they couldn't have survived the first few years of mothering twins without this group. Years later, many moms are still active members.) If you're not the club-joining type, online forums such as the message boards through *Twins* magazine (twins-magazine.com) can be a lifesaver. Even if these women can't offer you the exact solutions to the problem you may be experiencing, having someone else who knows what you're going through is often enough to make you feel better. Unfortunately, there's no national group for fathers of twins at this time, yet many have found welcoming support on *Twins* magazine message boards. If the dad of your multiples needs a bit of nurturing and assurance, encourage him to check them out.

The Identity Quest

If twins or triplets all fly the nest at once, it can be particularly hard on Mom (and sometimes Dad, too), especially if the multiples are her only children. For eighteen-plus years, she's been known as the mother of twins or triplets, and now her role is coming to an end, or so it seems. Many moms in this position feel a loss of identity. Their status has dwindled. Since so much of a parent's life has been wrapped up in her multiples, basking in the attention as the parent of twins, experts advise these parents to prepare for the day when their children leave much in the same way one prepares for retirement. Although it's important for parents to be involved and invested in their children's lives, it's equally important for them to have a life outside of the twin parameters. While multiples are busy studying and socializing in high school, moms and dads should slowly shift their priorities from their children to finding hobbies and activities they can enjoy solo or as husband and wife. Start by finding a passion—sports, art, music, literature—and take the time each week to invest in it. Just as you rebalance your financial portfolio once you approach retirement, parents of multiples should reconfigure their social priorities.

A mom of triplets told me she often thinks of the day her high school girls will leave home. As much as it pains her, she

> ### From One Parent to Another
>
> "A lot of the insight and memory comes from attending Mothers of Twins and Triplets groups, where you pass along your own experiences to new moms. There was a time when, once they (DZOS) passed a stage, I would forget stuff. Now members are amazed at how very much I do remember. It is a positive in another way, at sixty-eight years old, it keeps the brain working and keeps my thoughts young with the memories."

continues to encourage them to find their own adult voices. "Every time they go out on their own, they're one step closer to being adults."

How Twins Affect a Marriage

For most families, the arrival of multiples is seen as a bonus. Many husbands and wives handle the added stress of newborn multiples by banding together and taking on the attitude of "for better or worse," strengthening their commitment to one another in the process. Yes, the birth of multiples is definitely a double, triple, or even quadruple blessing, but it can also exert a lot of added stress on a marriage. Unfortunately, for some couples the stress is just too great to overcome and sadly their marriage dissolves. Let's be clear—multiples are not necessarily the cause of a marriage breaking up. More than likely there were deep-rooted problems within the union before the kids ever came along. The added strain of having multiples simply brought their preexisting troubles to the forefront.

Statistics do show that families with multiples have a higher divorce rate than families with single-born children. It doesn't take a rocket scientist to figure out the cause either: a marriage is especially vulnerable when the twins are babies and the stress of caring for two infants at once can intensify problems already existing in the marriage. Dad, although spending much more time at home helping to care for his new children, feels the added burden of providing for them. He has two careers now— one at home and one at the office—and is basically burning the candle at both ends. His wife, too, is exhausted from the constant care of two infants and in many cases has a professional career of her own. Economics play a role in how the family copes as well. If the couple was struggling financially prior to the arrival of twins, now the tension increases with the double expenses and ability to cope diminishes. Parents in this situation don't have the will or desire to support each other. They're both too busy just trying to keep their heads above water, and the result is a lonely and isolated couple. Many rebound successfully; others do not.

In troubled families, some parents develop a stronger affinity with one twin very early on. If a husband and wife don't feel connected to one another, they may end up looking to their children for the emotional warmth and companionship lacking in their own relationship. If these parent-and-child alliances continue through the years, they can form an unspoken dividing line—a riff—within the family. It can break up not only the marital dyad but the twin relationship as well, especially in a family where the twins are the only children.

What Parents Can Do

Having multiples is not all gloom and doom for your marriage, but the point is clear—prepare both mentally and economically for their arrival and seek help wherever and whenever you can. Here are a few guidelines to help.

- Never allow your multiples to "choose sides" with either parent. At the same time, never try to get one of your multiples to take your side against your spouse. Try to keep your marital disagreements private, and if you do argue in front of your children, let them see that it has been resolved successfully. "Yes, Daddy and I disagreed over the cost of the new refrigerator, but we talked about it and worked it out."
- Divide up household tasks. One of the biggest problems a marriage may face when multiples come along is when it feels as though the extra work all falls on one person. It may not, mind you, but each parent feels that he or she is carry-

ing the brunt of the new workload. Instead of feeling resentful, sit down with each other and first list what each does on a regular basis, including working outside the home, and then divide up household tasks accordingly.

- Make your marriage a priority. If there is a problem, admit it and seek professional help.

Making Marriage Merry Again

The union between a husband and wife is the most important relationship within the family. If the marriage dyad breaks apart, it can adversely affect everyone. Therefore, keeping your marriage healthy is vital. Yet to most of us, the secrets to a happy marriage can seem elusive and tricky at times. Here are a few pointers to put your marriage on the front burner.

- Focus on the positive qualities in your marriage. Praise the good. ("Hey, thanks for cleaning up the kitchen.") Try to overlook the annoying. (So what if you pick up the sweat socks and put them in the hamper every evening?) Remember to say "please," "thank you," and of course, "I love you." Show more affection toward each other—hold hands, give hugs freely, even an occasional squeeze builds a connection between husband and wife.
- Make time to talk alone. Set aside thirty minutes before or after dinner a few times a week to catch up with each other on the day-to-day stuff as well as your dreams for the future. Do it while the children are otherwise engaged (this is when TV is not so bad).
- Get out of the house together. Yes, date. I know that babysitting costs an arm and a leg and the typical evening excursion can easily run more than one hundred dollars, but you need to reconnect with your spouse, and the only way to do so is out of earshot of the kids. To offset the cost of babysitting, trade off duties with another family down the street. The rules are simple—drop the kids off at 4 P.M. and

Making Marriage Merry Again *(continued)*

pick them up by 9 P.M. No babysitting bills to pay, no bedtime dramas for the babysitter to battle, dating parents leave money for the pizza. And one more thing—when you finally do go out, don't talk about problems within the marriage but instead keep the conversation lively by talking about what makes your partnership special.

- Heat up your love life. This is the biggest predictor of marital satisfaction for men. Take the TV out of your bedroom! Furthermore, make the master bedroom your adult sanctuary. Create a space you want to retire to in the evening. In other words, spend a few bucks to make it not only comfortable but pleasurable for both of you, pleasing to the eye and soul. Some parents even have a "no kids allowed" policy in place from 8 P.M. on. That also means no kids in bed with you at night. Kids need to learn that there is a difference between family time and adult time.

ONE BIG, HAPPY FAMILY

The arrival of any child changes everything, and every marriage needs to adjust accordingly. Yet when multiples arrive on the scene, the family dynamics can take on new and different challenges for everyone—Mom, Dad, and even the single-born siblings. As you navigate through these new waters, remember that treating every member of the family as a special individual will help everyone feel equally important within the hierarchy. Remember, if you want all your children to appreciate and love one another, never play up the twin status at the expense of singletons in the household.

Bibliography

Many of the journals listed below can be found at university research libraries or accessed for a small fee through online services such as Ingenta Connect (ingentaconnect.com). Although some of the books listed below are no longer in print, they too can be found in university libraries or bought online through used booksellers such as Book Finder (bookfinder.com).

Åkerman, Britta Alin, and Eve Suurvee. "The Cognitive and Identity Development of Twins at Sixteen Years of Age: A Follow-up Study of Thirty-Two Twin Pairs." *Twin Research* 6 (2003): 328–333.

Bacon, Kate. "It's Good to Be Different: Parent and Child Negotiations of Twin Identity." *Twin Research and Human Genetics* 9 (2006): 141–147.

Bakker, Peter. "Autonomous Language of Twins." *Acta Geneticae Medicae et Gemellologiae* 36 (1987): 233–238.

Bank, Stephen, and Michael Kahn. *The Sibling Bond.* New York: Basic Books, 1997.

Bernabei, Paola, and Gabriel Levi. "Psychopathological Problems in Twins During Childhood." *Acta Geneticae Medicae et Gemellologiae* 25 (1976): 381–383.

Bouchard, Thomas, et al. "Sources of Human Psychological Differences: The Minnesota Study of Twins Reared Apart." *Science* 250, no. 4978 (1990): 223–229.

Claridge, Gordon, et al. *Personality Differences and Biological Variations: A Study of Twins*. Oxford: Pergamon Press, 1973.

Danby, Susan, and Karen Thorpe. "Compatibility and Conflict: Negotiation of Relationships by Dizygotic Same-Sex Twin Girls." *Twin Research and Human Genetics* 9 (2006): 103–112.

DiLalla, Lisabeth Fisher. "Social Development of Twins." *Twin Research and Human Genetics* 9 (2006): 95–102.

DiLalla, Lisabeth Fisher, and Rebecca Caraway. "Behavioral Inhibition as a Function of Relationship in Preschool Twins and Siblings." *Twin Research* 7 (2004): 449–455.

Ebeling, Hanna, et al. "Inter-Twin Relationships and Mental Health." *Twin Research* 6 (2003): 334–343.

El-Hai, Jack. "Uniquely Twins." *Minnesota Medicine* 82 (1999).

Faber, Adele, and Elaine Mazlish. *Siblings Without Rivalry: How to Help Your Children Live Together So You Can Live Too*. New York: Quill, 2002.

Gleeson, C., et al. "Twins in School: An Australia-Wide Program." *Acta Geneticae Medicae et Gemellologiae* 39 (1990): 231–244.

Hay, David. "ADHD and Multiples: A Family Affair." *Twins* 21, no. 5 (2004): 28–31.

Hay, David. "Twins in School: La Trobe Twins Study." Department of Psychology, La Trobe University, Melbourne, Australia, and Australian Multiple Birth Association Inc. (1991).

Hay, David, et al. "Speech and Language Development in Preschool Twins." *Acta Geneticae Medicae et Gemellologiae* 36 (1987): 213–223.

Hay, David, et al. "The High Incidence of Reading Disability in Twin Boys and Its Implications for Genetic Analyses." *Acta Geneticae Medicae et Gemellologiae* 33 (1984): 223–236.

Hay, David, and P. J. O'Brien. "Early Influences on the School Social Adjustment of Twins." *Acta Geneticae Medicae et Gemellologiae* 36 (1987): 239–248.

Hay, David, and P. J. O'Brien. "The Role of Parental Attitudes in the Development of Temperament in Twins at Home, School and in Test Situations." *Acta Geneticae Medicae et Gemellologiae* 33 (1984): 191–204.

Johnson, Wendy, et al. "The Personality of Twins: Just Ordinary Folks." *Twin Research* 5 (2002): 125–131.

Koch, Helen. *Twins and Twin Relations.* Chicago: University of Chicago Press, 1966.

Koeppen-Schomerus, Gesina, et al. "Twins and Non-Twin Siblings: Different Estimates of Shared Environment Influence in Early Childhood." *Twin Research* 6 (2003): 97–105.

Lennarstson, AmyJo. "Minnesota Twins Win." *Twins* 22, no. 4 (2005): 18–20.

Loehlin, John C. *Heredity, Environment and Personality: A Study of 850 Sets of Twins.* Austin: University of Texas Press, 1976.

Lytton, Hugh. *Parent-Child Interaction: The Socialisation Process Observed in Twins and Singleton Families.* New York: Plenum Press, 1980.

McClearn, Gerald, et al. "Substantial Genetic Influence on Cognitive Abilities in Twins Eighty or More Years Old." *Science* 276 (1997): 1560–1563.

McDougall, Megan, et al. "Having a Co-Twin with Attention-Deficit Hyperactivity Disorder." *Twin Research and Human Genetics* 9 (2006): 148–154.

Mittler, Peter. *The Study of Twins.* Middlesex: Penguin Books, 1971.

Moilanen, Irma. "Dominance and Submissiveness Between Twins." *Acta Geneticae Medicae et Gemellologiae* 36 (1987): 249–255.

Moilanen, Irma, and P. Rantakallio. "Living Habits and Personality Development of Adolescent Twins: A Longitudinal Follow-Up Study in a Birth Cohort from Pregnancy to Adolescence." *Acta Geneticae Medicae et Gemellologiae* 39 (1990): 215–220.

Pearlman, Eileen M., and Jill Alison Ganon. *Raising Twins: What Parents Want to Know (and What Twins Want to Tell Them).* New York: Collins, 2000.

Piontelli, Alessandra. *Twins: From Fetus to Child.* London: Routledge, 2002.

Posthuma, Daniëlle, et al. "Twin-Singleton Differences in Intelligence?" *Twin Research* 3 (2000): 83–87.

Pulkkinen, Lea, et al. "Peer Reports of Adaptive Behavior in Twins and Singletons: Is Twinship a Risk or an Advantage?" *Twin Research* 6 (2003): 106–118.

Rosambeau, Mary. *How Twins Grow Up*. London: The Bodley Head, 1987.

Sandbank, Audrey. "The Effects of Twins on Family Relationships." *Acta Geneticae Medicae et Gemellologiae* 37 (1988): 161–171.

Sandbank, Audrey. *Twins and the Family*. London: Arrow Books, 1988.

Sandbank, Audrey (editor). *Twins and Triplet Psychology: A Professional Guide to Working with Multiples*. London: Routledge, 1999.

Scheinfeld, Amram. *Twins and Supertwins*. Philadelphia: J. B. Lippincott Company, 1967.

Segal, Nancy, and Scott Hershberger. "Cooperation and Competition Between Twins: Findings from a Prisoner's Dilemma Game." *Evolution and Human Behavior* 20 (1999): 29–51.

Sheehan, Grania. "Adolescent Sibling Conflict: The Role of Parental Favouritism." *Family Matters* 46 (1997): 37–39.

Sheehan, Grania, and Patricia Noller. "Adolescents' Perceptions of Differential Parenting: Links with Attachment Style and Adolescent Adjustment." *Personal Relationships* 9 (2002): 173–190.

Smilansky, Sara. *Twins and Their Development: The Roles of Family and School*. Rockville: BJE Press, 1992.

Stewart, Elizabeth. "Towards the Social Analysis of Twinship." *British Journal of Sociology* 51 (2000): 719–737.

Thorpe, Karen. "Twins and Friendship." *Twin Research* 6 (2003): 532–535.

Thorpe, Karen, and Susan Danby. "Compromised or Competent: Analyzing Twin Children's Social Worlds." *Twin Research and Human Genetics* 9 (2006): 90–94.

Thorpe, Karen, and Karen Gardner. "Twins and Their Friendships: Differences Between Monozygotic, Dizygotic Same-Sex and Dizygotic Mixed-Sex Pairs." *Twin Research and Human Genetics* 9 (2006): 155–164.

Torgersen, Anne Mari, and Harald Janson. "Why Do Identical Twins Differ in Personality: Shared Environment Reconsidered." *Twin Research* 5 (2002): 44–52.

Trias, L. Tuulikki, et al. "How Long Do the Consequences of Parental Preference Last: A Study of Twins from Pregnancy to Young

Adulthood." *Twin Research and Human Genetics* 9 (2006): 240–249.

Trouton, Alexandra, et al. "Twins Early Development Study (TEDS): A Multivariate, Longitudinal Genetic Investigation of Language, Cognition and Behavior Problems in Childhood." *Twin Research* 5 (2002): 444–448.

Tully, Lucy, et al. "What Effect Does Classroom Separation Have on Twins' Behavior, Progress at School, and Reading Abilities?" *Twin Research* 7 (2004): 115–224.

Van Leeuwen, Marieke, et al. "Effects of Twin Separation in Primary School." *Twin Research and Human Genetics* 8 (2005): 384–391.

Wadsworth, Sally, and John DeFries. "Genetic Etiology of Reading Difficulties in Boys and Girls." *Twin Research and Human Genetics* 8 (2005): 594–601.

Walker, Sheila, et al. "Nature, Nurture and Academic Achievement: A Twin Study of Teacher Assessments of Seven-Year-Olds." *British Journal of Educational Psychology* 74 (2004): 323–342.

Wright, Lawrence. *Twins: And What They Tell Us About Who We Are*. New York: John Wiley & Sons, 1997.

Yoon, Young-Soon, and Yoon-Mi Hur. "Twins Have Slightly Higher Self-Concepts Than Singletons in the Elementary School Period: A Study of South Korean Twins and Singletons." *Twin Research and Human Genetics* 9 (2006): 233–239.

Zazzo, Rene. "The Twin Condition and the Couple Effects on Personality Development." *Acta Geneticae Medicae et Gemellologiae* 25 (1976): 343–352.

Index